D1467734

The Neanderthals

LIFE WORLD LIBRARY
LIFE NATURE LIBRARY
TIME READING PROGRAM
THE LIFE HISTORY OF THE UNITED STATES
LIFE SCIENCE LIBRARY
GREAT AGES OF MAN
TIME-LIFE LIBRARY OF ART
TIME-LIFE LIBRARY OF AMERICA
FOODS OF THE WORLD
THIS FABULOUS CENTURY
LIFE LIBRARY OF PHOTOGRAPHY
THE TIME-LIFE ENCYCLOPEDIA OF GARDENING
THE AMERICAN WILDERNESS
THE EMERGENCE OF MAN
THE OLD WEST
FAMILY LIBRARY:
   THE TIME-LIFE BOOK OF FAMILY FINANCE
   THE TIME-LIFE FAMILY LEGAL GUIDE

The Emergence of Man

The Neanderthals

by George Constable
and the Editors
of Time-Life Books

Time-Life Books
New York

The Author: GEORGE CONSTABLE, a member of the staff of TIME-LIFE BOOKS, has written extensively on scientific subjects. He has also written three novels, *All the Abandoned Children, The Imaginocrats* and *What Shy Men Dream,* as well as several children's books, including *The Whale Hunters* and *Warrior Knights.*

The Consultant: RALPH S. SOLECKI, Professor of Anthropology at Columbia University, is an authority on Neanderthal man. A graduate of City College of New York and Columbia, he was formerly with the Smithsonian Institution. His book *Shanidar, The First Flower People* describes his dig at a Neanderthal site in Iraq.

The Cover: Two Neanderthals, returning from a hunt, pause warily as they pick their way through a pile of lichen-splotched boulders deposited by a glacier over 40,000 years ago. The first—and most controversial—of the ancient men to be found, they were not apish brutes, as long thought, but large-brained predecessors of modern man who fashioned tools, clothes and shelters to survive the rigors of the ice age.

The cover scene, as well as those on pages 29-37, has been re-created by painting Neanderthals on photographs of types of landscapes known to have existed during Neanderthal times. The cover artist was Burt Silverman; Herb Steinberg provided the figures for pages 29-37.

Contents

Introduction

To most people Neanderthal man is anything but human—a grunting, shuffling beast rather than an intelligent being. But recently a true picture of him has taken shape, and a different picture it is from the one commonly held. Within less than a generation of our own lifetime this ancient man has been lifted from the misconceptions of nearly a century to deserved inclusion within the ranks of humanity.

The revised picture came about when new research —and long, critical looks at old research (most of it badly done by present standards)—yielded the conclusion that Neanderthal man was really not so much different from us. The major differences appear to be of degree rather than kind. Viewing the total picture of Neanderthal, we see what in effect is the mind of modern man locked into the body of an archaic creature. The basis for this more appreciative view comes from discoveries of Neanderthals' beliefs, customs and rituals. Burial of the dead, compassion for fellow men and attempts to control destiny were aspects of life new with Neanderthals; they cared, a human phenomenon totally fresh in the emergence of man. If there is anything that can be labeled as of paramount importance in human development, aside from the evolution of the brain itself, it is the appearance of caring. But the mind of modern man also brings undesirable characteristics, and we can see the price of mental advancement in Neanderthal fossils: some skeletons show the signs of deliberately inflicted wounds, the result of human violence.

As this book shows, during the time of the Neanderthals, 40,000 to about 100,000 years ago, invention and discovery were beginning to be felt in a changing world, alternately gripped in the frost and thaw of the ice ages. Neanderthal man expanded far beyond the confining territorial bounds of his predecessor, Homo erectus, tentatively thrusting into the colder areas of the northland on the one hand and into the steaming forest areas on the other. To cope with often difficult environments, he became a highly skilled stone artisan, and the delicacy of his workmanship can be appreciated only when we attempt to duplicate his stone tools.

There is of course much that we do not know about the Neanderthals, because all that we have to go on are stones and bones and traces left in the soil where these people camped or lived. We really do not know if a Neanderthal man had a full beard, or if he had sparse facial covering like some contemporary races. Moreover, we do not know if his skin was light or dark. And yet in spite of gaps in our knowledge, I, as an anthropologist and archeologist whose field researches in the Near East have been intimately tied up with studies of Neanderthal man for over 20 years, find my appreciation of him ever mounting. When I first began excavation of a cave that Neanderthals had occupied in Iraq, my position was that of an impartial observer, tallying up the count of their material effects, recording the depths of deposits and noting down other technical details. But the recovery of the bones of the Neanderthals who had made or used the objects gave me a new understanding of these people. When I realized that a particular human brain, eye and hand had been involved in the production of the flints I held, they suddenly acquired a very personal touch. And then, when a Neanderthal burial in the same cave turned out to have been accompanied by the flowers of mourners, the last barrier of understanding between me and Neanderthal man broke down. He stepped forward, a whole man.

Ralph S. Solecki

Chapter One: The Ancestor Nobody Wanted

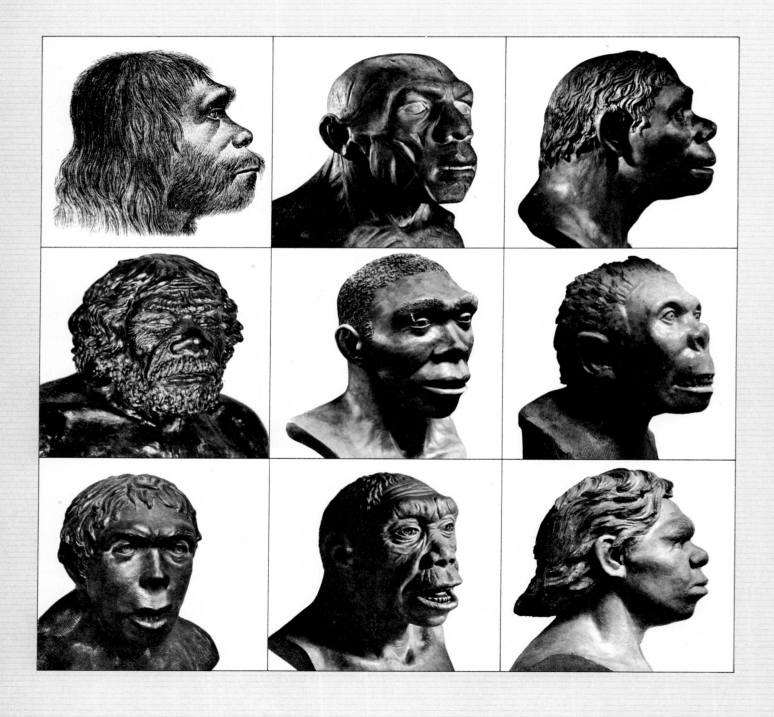

Neanderthal. The word is familiar enough. Most modern men have a vague impression that it refers to a shambling, beetle-browed lout who prowled the earth during the Ice Age, wearing ragged furs, speaking in grunts and occasionally pausing to bat a woman over the head with a club and drag her back to his cave. In popular usage, the word is a stinging insult. Calling someone a Neanderthal is close to legally actionable slander.

The Neanderthals got such a poor reputation among the general public because they were grievously misjudged by the experts. Until recently, almost all paleoanthropologists regarded Neanderthals as a brutish breed that at best represented an insignificant side branch of the human family tree. Only now is this misjudgment being remedied. It turns out that although the Neanderthals were indeed different from modern man, they were sufficiently human in mind and body to deserve modern man's own species name, Homo sapiens. Even more important, there is much new evidence to demonstrate that some Neanderthals—and perhaps all of them—were our immediate ancestors; they carried the torch of evolution during the millennia from 100,000 years ago to about 40,000 years ago. During this period they greatly expanded the regions occupied by man, devised ingenious stone tools to exploit nature, and opened the

A gallery of portraits of Neanderthal man dating from 1888 (top left) shows how widely conceptions of him have varied —even when based on the same fossil find. The reconstruction with its musculature exposed (top center) was modeled in the early 20th Century for the noted French anthropologist Marcellin Boule (pages 19-22) from a skull found at La Chapelle-aux-Saints. Other scientists took the same skull and, reconstructing the soft tissue differently, came up with the heads in the second row at left and at bottom right.

door onto the world of the supernatural. Clearly, they were ancestors to be proud of.

Why did the experts misjudge the Neanderthals? Many reasons could be cited—the scarcity of fossils, errors in reconstructing bone fragments and other technical difficulties. But perhaps more important, these problems were compounded by an accident of timing. The Neanderthals made their appearance midway through the 19th Century, at a critical moment in intellectual history, when old but comfortable ideas about the human past were beginning to fall apart and new but shocking ideas—such as evolution—were coming in. The old ideas could not explain the Neanderthals. The new ones, which could, were generally unwelcome and almost always poorly understood. Thus, no one was prepared for the actual sight of a primitive-looking skeleton in the human closet, and when such a skeleton appeared in Germany in 1856, it brought on a crippling case of ancestor-blindness. A full century would pass before scientists recovered from this malady.

Neanderthal man first turned up not far from the city of Düsseldorf, Germany, where a tributary stream of the Rhine flows through a steep-sided gorge known as the Neander Valley—*Neanderthal* in Old German. In 1856 the flanks of the gorge were being quarried for limestone. During the summer, workmen blasted open a small cave about 60 feet above the stream. As they dug their pickaxes into the floor of the cave, they uncovered a number of ancient bones. But the quarrymen were intent on limestone; they did not pay much attention to the bones, and most of what was probably a complete skeleton of a Neanderthal was lost. Only the skullcap, ribs, part of the pelvis and some limb bones were saved.

The owner of the quarry thought that these fragments belonged to a bear, and he presented them to the local science teacher, J. K. Fuhlrott, who was known to be interested in such things. Fuhlrott had enough anatomical knowledge to realize that the skeletal remains came not from a bear but from a man —and a most extraordinary man at that. The thickness of the limbs and the heavy, slanted brow of the skullcap seemed very ancient to him. In an attempt to account for the apparent antiquity and odd location of the relics, he concluded that they belonged to some poor mortal who had been washed into the cave by Noah's flood.

Knowing that this judgment was bound to be disputed, he called in an expert, Hermann Schaaffhausen, professor of anatomy at the University of Bonn. Schaaffhausen agreed that the bones represented one of the "most ancient races of man." He had in mind an age of no more than a few thousand years, thinking that the fossil fragments could have come from some barbarian who had lived in northern Europe before the Celtic and Germanic tribes arrived. It never occurred to Schaaffhausen that these bones belonged to a much older individual, distinct from any known race, barbarian or not.

Schaaffhausen can hardly be faulted for missing the truth about the man from the Neander Valley. In 1856 the scientific community did not realize that humankind had been on earth for any substantial length of time. And no respectable scientist believed that humans had ever existed in any form other than that of modern man. Such a notion would have been directly contrary to the scheme known as the Chain of Being, the framework for biological thought since the time of Aristotle. The Chain of Being was a grandly conceived hierarchy for all living things. Every creature had a rank. Starting with the lowliest worm, the hierarchy progressed steadily upward through ever more advanced species and finally reached the pinnacle of life—man himself. Creatures positioned close to each other on this chain naturally showed some similarities—and even man admittedly resembled apes in his outward form (although his mental and spiritual capacities were regarded as being infinitely superior). But similarity between types of creatures did not mean that there was any family connection. The separate links of the Chain of Being were thought to have been fixed in perpetuity at the Creation; species never changed and certainly never evolved from lowlier forms.

This orderly scheme still held sway in 1856, but it was being shaken by the appearance of animal bones unlike those of any living creatures, suggesting to some maverick thinkers that the Chain of Being did not tell the full story of life. Most authorities dismissed the problem. They ascribed the anomalous bones to the "sportiveness" of God, or contended that several separate Creations had occurred in the past. But extinct animals were not the only threat to the scheme. A few primitive-looking human fossils had been found as early as the year 1700, and probably on many occasions before that. What are now known to be Neanderthal remains had been uncovered in Belgium in 1829 and on the north face of Gibraltar in 1848. However, unlike the man from the Neander Valley, these finds received no publicity, and science was not forced to grapple with their significance.

On one crucial question concerning the past—its length—science had already accepted some major revisions by the mid-19th Century. During the previous century, the prevailing view of the past was based on the Book of Genesis, which indicated that the world had been created in six days about 6,000 years before. But even in the 18th Century a few perceptive men felt that the earth had to be much older. One of them, an amateur English geologist, James Hutton, theorized that the surface features visible on the earth—mountains, plains, oceans—could be accounted for only if the planet had undergone repeated change, the earth being lifted up and then eroded. To produce the changes he saw, the geological forces must have been at work for a long time; Hutton accordingly rejected the Biblical timetable for the origin of the world, declaring that "we find no vestige of a beginning, no prospect of an end."

Practically all contemporary authorities disagreed with Hutton, if they ever heard of him at all. At most, they conceded that the features of the planet might have been altered a few times during prehistory by cataclysmic events—floods, collisions with comets, and so on. But in the 1830s, another English geologist, Charles Lyell, adduced masses of evidence showing that the earth was being constantly reshaped by complex geological processes and had been in existence for millions of years.

Lyell's proof of the great age of the earth caused many people to wonder where humankind had been during those epochs of geological change. The easiest answer, and the one still generally accepted when the Neanderthal fossil appeared, was that humans had been created rather recently. An alternative explanation consigned humans to refuge in the Garden of Eden. But these pleasant notions about the comparative youthfulness of humankind were about to be replaced by a vision of hoary age.

This reversal of expert opinion came only two years after the Neanderthal fossil turned up. But old Neanderthal's bones had nothing to do with the turnabout in doctrine. The evidence that first convinced scientists that humans had been present on earth for a very long time—and had, in fact, left voluminous records of their presence—was stone tools. Farmers, road builders and practically anyone who dug into the ground had been finding these tools for centuries but had not realized what they were. The objects, instead of being interpreted as the handiwork of ancient, culturally undeveloped men, were regarded as freak products of nature—of humidity, solar radiation or, most likely of all, lightning. A popular name for them was thunderstones, and some French and Scandinavian farmers placed them in the walls or under the doorsills of their houses to ward off lightning, on the dubious theory that it never struck twice in the same place.

During the 1830s, a French customs inspector named Boucher de Perthes discerned the truth about the implements. He had found chunks of chipped stone in the gravel terraces of the Somme River Valley in northwestern France. As he collected and sorted the stones in a systematic manner, noting their points and edges, he became convinced that they were tools, made by men. Judging by their position below the surface, he felt that they pre-dated recorded history. His findings were published in several volumes, but were greeted with general scorn in France. Finally, in 1858, a group of British scientists decided to take a firsthand look at the evidence —something their French colleagues had not bothered to do. They visited the site and concluded that De Perthes was absolutely right. (He was more right

Making a Monkey out of Man

Darwinian Man,
though well-behaved
At best
is only a monkey shaved.

This sarcastic verse, from a Gilbert and Sullivan operetta of 1884, and the 19th Century cartoons reproduced here, are relatively mild expressions of the shocked disbelief that greeted Darwin's publication of the theory of evolution—and so confused the meaning of Neanderthal man, discovered about the same time, that his true significance is only now being grasped. Darwin had hoped that the doctrine of natural selection would throw light on the origin of modern man; what it did throw was a thunderbolt. Complacent Victorians refused to accept the idea that humans had ever looked different, or that Neanderthal could be their ancestor.

Almost all critics of evolution misunderstood Darwin and assumed he meant that modern man is directly descended from an ape or monkey. Even the open-minded British statesman Benjamin Disraeli seemed to echo this misconception when he suggested that Darwin had raised a question whether man was an ape or an angel, and proclaimed himself "on the side of the angels." The battle over evolution has not ended. In 1972 California's Board of Education was torn by a dispute over a proposal that children should be taught the Biblical version of "creation by design" as well as evolution. That proposal lost, but the Board refused to accept unquestioning espousal of evolution.

Human evolution was ridiculed in this 1872 cartoon, satirizing On the Origin of Species by showing man's descent from pig to bull to man.

Darwin, inviting an ape to jump through the hoop, was identified as the "wise father that knows his own son."

Society's new member—thanks to Darwin—is announced by a shocked butler: "Mr. Gg-g-o-o-o-rilla!"

One caged monkey requests another in an 1876 Harper's Bazaar to amputate his tail so that he can more quickly take on his august role as a man.

Weeping monkeys mourn the death of their benefactor, Charles Darwin, in an 1882 issue of the Viennese magazine Kikeriki. With Darwin passed away, moan the monkeys, who will now be our defender and champion our cause?

An ape sandwich man poses the fundamental, much-debated question of the century, however oversimplified and humorized, for Britain's Punch magazine in 1871.

A cruel caricature of Darwin, which appeared in The Hornet in 1871, labeled him "a venerable orang-outang" and cited his contribution to "unnatural history."

than he knew; the stone tools that he had found were at least 300,000 years old.)

Then, one year after the British delegation had validated De Perthes' work and officially endowed mankind with a dizzyingly extensive past, the scientific world was rocked to its foundations by the publication of a book, *On the Origin of Species,* by Charles Darwin. With the appearance of this volume, the tidy scheme of the Chain of Being was undone. Darwin showed that plant and animal species were not permanent but were capable of changing and giving rise to new forms. He also showed that the geological record holds proof of the evolutionary progress of life from lower to higher forms. Darwin said almost nothing about the possibility of man's arising from a lower form (his reticence did not prevent one angry Welshman from writing a letter calling him a hairy old ape). Yet evidence for such a revolutionary conclusion was in existence—the fossil dug from the cave in Germany. Here was a man who looked different from any man then living, even more different than a Norwegian from a Hottentot. And the scientific community knew about this specimen. Schaaffhausen had seen to that. He had published an article about the bones and had displayed them to a number of scientific societies.

Still the hint fell on deaf ears. No one accepted the Neanderthal as a human ancestor. Almost no one was willing to admit that the fossil was ancient. The consensus was that the Neanderthal bones came from a standard-model human being whose strange characteristics were attributable to disease or "foreignness." A number of researchers produced hypotheses that sound like forerunners of today's ethnic jokes. One German anatomist looked at the somewhat bowed leg bones and suggested that they belonged to a man who had spent a lifetime on horseback. With dazzling specificity, he ventured a guess that the fossil man was a Mongolian Cossack of the Russian cavalry, which had chased Napoleon back across the Rhine in 1814; he further guessed that the Cossack had deserted the Russian forces and later crawled into the Neander Valley cave to die. Another anatomist studied the low-vaulted skullcap and thought he glimpsed the lineaments of "an old Dutchman." A French scientist weighed in with the opinion that this skull came from "a powerfully organized Celt . . . with low mental organization."

Still another scholar, eschewing the temptation to dismiss the fossil as some sort of low-grade foreigner, observed that the bones came from a man who had suffered from rickets and who had also broken an elbow that never fully healed. He was correct about these defects, but unfortunately he then moved on to a staggering deduction about the formation of the skull. He surmised that the constant pain of the man's afflictions caused him to knot his brow in anguish; eventually the agonized expression became ossified, producing the ridge of bone over the eyes.

In England experts displayed a bit more sobriety. The geologist Lyell visited Germany and brought a cast of the Neanderthal skull back to London, where it was exhibited between the skulls of a gorilla and a Negro—a reflection of the racial attitudes of the day. His colleague Thomas Huxley, a forceful champion of Darwin's new theory of evolution, acknowledged that this skull was the most apelike he had ever come across, but "in no sense can the Neanderthal bones be regarded as the remains of a human being intermediate between men and apes."

Only Dr. William King, professor of anatomy at Queen's College in Galway, Ireland, accepted the fossil as an extinct form of humanity. He suggested that the specimen be placed in a separate species, *Homo neanderthalensis.* In giving the fossil the genus name of *Homo,* King was acknowledging a general similarity to humankind; but he felt that he could not add the species name for modern man—*sapiens,* derived from the Latin word for "wise"—because, as he wrote, "The Neanderthal skull is so eminently simian . . . I am constrained to believe that the thoughts and desires which once dwelt within it never soared beyond those of the brute."

King's assessment was closer to being correct than anyone else's, but he later changed his thinking when he heard what Rudolf Virchow, a famed German anatomist-anthropologist, had to say. In a closely reasoned paper, Virchow stated that the man from the Neander Valley was not ancient at all, but a modern Homo sapiens who had suffered from rickets in childhood and arthritis in old age, and had also received several stupendous blows on the head at some time during his life. This pronouncement, coming from such a respected source, effectively silenced all further speculation.

How could these authorities conclude that the Neanderthal bones were modern? The incompleteness of the fossil was one factor: because the skull lacked a face and a jaw, it was hard to tell what the man had looked like. Also, no one could say for certain that the Neanderthal man was really old since no stone tools or bones of extinct animals had accompanied the fossil. Without proof of great age, it was thought best to err on the side of caution and presume a date not too remote from the present. Nor would it be fair to indict the cautious scientists of the day for inclining toward the safest position. Those who accepted the theories of Darwin and De Perthes were open-minded by any standard. It took a large measure of intellectual courage to surrender the accepted wisdom of centuries for Darwin's brave new world of evolution.

The Darwinists, to their great credit, were actively interested in discovering a less advanced human ancestor from the moment that *On the Origin of Species* appeared. But it must be remembered that they had no way of knowing where to look. Huxley, a bold and brilliant man, believed that there was little hope of finding fossils that would reveal human evolutionary history. Some of the evolutionists did not even think that it was necessary to peer into the past. They believed that the present offered examples of men who were intermediate between themselves and some primitive ancestral form. One presumed authority suggested that Negroes displayed intermediate traits. He claimed that the Negro "rarely stands quite upright" and that his foot has prehensile tendencies, like apes. This same man also pointed to mental institutions: "I do not hesitate to uphold . . . that microcephali and born idiots present as perfect a series from man to ape as may be wished for." Such surmises received only slight approval, but they do suggest why the evolutionary significance of Neanderthal man was overlooked. Even supposedly clear-eyed scientists often see what they expect to see. They did not expect evolutionary intermediates to turn up in a cave, hence they never really gave the evidence a fair chance.

As soon as Virchow had announced that the odd appearance of the bones from the Neander Valley

J. K. Fuhlrott, *first to recognize Neanderthal's significance, was shown the initial discovery because he taught science to the child of the man whose workers had discovered the fossil remains. He later became a professor.*

Hermann Schaaffhausen, *who firmly believed that the bones belonged to an ancient man, was for 50 years a professor at the University of Bonn popular for his lectures. He bought the fossils for the local museum.*

Charles Lyell, *founder of modern geology, proved the earth was millions of years old—thus suggesting that man, too, was ancient. To further study of Neanderthal in England, he went to Germany for a cast of the skull.*

was a result of disease rather than antiquity, the fossil ceased to disturb scientists. They simply forgot about it. However, prehistorians were still very much interested in finding an ancient fossil ancestor of modern man—on one condition. The fossil had to look like a modern man; anything that resembled an animal ancestor—an ape or monkey—was almost automatically rejected.

This curious standard for acceptance was demonstrated when a new fossil appeared in 1868. Near a hill known as Cro-Magnon in southwestern France, workmen who were preparing a roadbed for a railway uncovered an ancient rock shelter—an overhanging ledge that could fend off rain or snow. Digging down through the deposits of earth beneath the rock shelter, they came across flint tools, broken animal bone—and the remains of five individuals.

One male skeleton was almost complete. Aside from a certain robustness, it closely resembled modern man. The skull had a high vault, a vertical face and a prominent chin. Yet the presence of stone tools and bones of extinct animals left no doubt that the man had lived long ago. He was welcomed into the human family tree almost immediately. He was no heavy-limbed, beetle-browed brute but a tall, lordly fellow. It was easy to imagine him surveying the landscape with piercing eyes and leading his band of hunters in combat against the fierce beasts of his snow-mantled world. The "Old Man of Cro-Magnon," as he was called, seemed to confirm that humans had always looked the way they do today—and he stirred a general sense of relief.

But this uneasy accommodation to the past was disrupted when, in 1886, additional fossils appeared

William King, *first to come to the conclusion that the Neanderthal fossils were actually the relics of an extinct human species different from the modern one, was a professor of geology at Queen's College, Galway, Ireland.*

Rudolf Virchow *was a brilliant but bull-headed professor at the University of Berlin. Though founding father of the science of pathology, Virchow nevertheless insisted Neanderthal was a modern man with a bashed-in skull.*

Marcellin Boule *was the early 20th Century's foremost authority on fossils and traveled the world to study new finds. Yet he created a badly distorted reconstruction of Neanderthal that misled scientists for many decades.*

—primitive-looking ones. A cave near an area called Spy in Belgium yielded two skeletons. One skull, probably from a female, was reminiscent of the original fossil from the Neander Valley in Germany, although the cranium was higher and the forehead somewhat less slanted. The other skull was virtually identical to the fossil from Germany. Coincidence? Yes, said Rudolf Virchow. He dismissed the Spy skeletons as further diseased specimens of modern man. But this explanation began to sound hollow. Not only was such a coincidence of pathological deformity most unlikely but these fossils were definitely very old—as indicated by the primitive stone tools and the remains of extinct animals found with them. Most scientists were obliged to admit that an archaic people, distinct from modern man, had indeed lived in Europe during some bygone era.

The Spy skeletons lacked some parts, but they were complete enough to serve as models for a rough sketch of Neanderthals. In stature, these people were short and thickset. Their heads were long and low, with large brow ridges. Their faces were massive and outthrust, with a heavy jaw but a receding chin. Were they our ancestors? Did Homo sapiens, the finest flower of creation, arise from this stock? Nearly all scientists said no. They were willing to accord Neanderthal a place on the human family tree but not on a branch shared by modern man. Some authorities felt that the Neanderthals might represent an aberrant offshoot from the main evolutionary line; if they were related to true men at all, they were poor and distant relatives.

Then an even more primitive-looking fossil came to light in 1891. Pithecanthropus, a big-jawed, small-brained creature, was found in Java. What was the connection between Pithecanthropus (later known as Homo erectus) and the bigger-brained Neanderthals of Belgium and Germany? Most experts saw no connection, but a few theorists attempted a bold synthesis. They suggested that both Pithecanthropus and the Neanderthals deserved to be placed right on the trunk of the family tree. Their reasoning went this way: three main kinds of fossils, all apparently very ancient, had appeared—Pithecanthropus, the Neanderthals and Cro-Magnon man. Pithecanthropus looked the most primitive, the Neanderthals somewhat less so, and the Cro-Magnon specimen was completely modern. Thus, logic suggested that human evolution had passed through three separate stages, represented by the three distinct fossil types. As if to reinforce this conclusion, a massive jawbone was found in a sand pit near Heidelberg, Germany, in 1907; it seemed to show that Pithecanthropus had lived in Europe prior to the time of the Neanderthals and Cro-Magnons.

Now the Neanderthals were beginning to interest people again. The initial shocked reaction to Darwin's theory of evolution was over. The discomfiting notion that man had been around for tens or hundreds of thousands of years was becoming accepted. The fossils from Spy indicated that the Neanderthals were ancient men, not modern ones deformed by disease. And the discovery of small-brained Pithecanthropus helped put the Neanderthals in perspective. Although most experts were not yet willing to trace man's lineage through a Neanderthal stage of evolution, their belief that humankind could never have looked as primitive as a Neanderthal was now main-

ly a subjective feeling, and thus open to debate. But just at this point, when the riddle of man's ancestry seemed about to be solved, new evidence muddled the problem almost hopelessly.

In the first decade of the 20th Century, paleoanthropologists were hard at work in the Dordogne region of southwestern France. The Dordogne seems to have been a sort of Promised Land for prehistoric man, even during the epochs of bitter glacial cold that gripped Europe from time to time. Many millions of years ago this area was covered by a warm sea. Tiny lime-containing marine organisms died and settled on the sea floor, producing thick deposits of limestone; much later, the sea bottom was lifted high and dry. The resulting limestone plateau was gradually eroded into a maze of hills and canyons where great herds of animals roamed. And the region also offered excellent shelter to hunters, because a warren of caves had been created where ground water dissolved the limestone.

From the 1860s on, countless stone tools were found in the Dordogne, proof that it had been a population center in ancient times. Beginning in the year 1908 a magnificent series of Neanderthal fossils was discovered. One of the first to turn up was the skeleton of an old man in a cave near the village of La Chapelle-aux-Saints. A nearby cave at Le Moustier, from which quantities of stone implements had been excavated earlier, yielded the skeleton of a Neanderthal youth. A rock shelter at La Ferrassie produced an adult male Neanderthal and later the remains of several children. Another rock shelter at La Quina held parts of several Neanderthal skeletons.

The great value of the Dordogne material was its completeness. Up to this point scientists had been struggling with fragments. The bones from Spy had sufficed for a rough portrait of these early men, but as long as the look of the Neanderthals remained at all hazy, venturesome scholars could leap to extremes and see them as either Homo sapiens or gorillas. (One German anthropologist did, in fact, believe that the Neanderthals were descended from a creature resembling a gorilla, but his theory held a curious corollary: he felt that Homo sapiens was descended on a parallel line from a creature resembling an orangutan.) However, the wealth of skeletal material from southwestern France seemed to spell an end to this anthropological free-for-all. Now scientists would be able to study the physical resemblances—or lack thereof—between Neanderthals and modern man.

The man from La Chapelle-aux-Saints was selected for a detailed reconstruction of a typical Neanderthal—a task which fell to a French expert named Marcellin Boule of the French National Museum of Natural History. Boule was a paleontologist, a specialist in the study of old bones. On this project, he had an unusually fine set of bones to work with. The materials were well preserved, and although some of the bones were broken, almost everything of importance was available except some teeth and vertebrae. Yet Boule proceeded to commit an astonishing series of errors—and they were not corrected for decades.

Boule so misconstructed the bones as to make the Neanderthal appear much like an ape from head to toe. He mistakenly arranged the foot bones so that the big toe diverged from the other toes like an opposable thumb; this feature presumably forced the Neanderthal to walk on the outer part of his feet, like an ape. Boule's interpretation of the knee joint was equally incorrect: he declared that the Neander-thal could not fully extend his leg, and that this resulted in a bent-knee gait.

In every respect, the posture of Boule's reconstruction seemed nonhuman. According to Boule, the spine lacked the curves that allow modern man to stand upright. Atop this misshapen spine the head was placed in an unbalanced position, thrust so far forward that the Neanderthal probably would have sprained his neck if he had tried to look at the sky. If Boule's Neanderthal man resembled any kind of man at all, it was a shuffling hunchback.

But the most devastating conclusion of the study focused on the intelligence of the man from La Chapelle-aux-Saints. Boule ignored the fossil's large cranial capacity. He looked only at the long, low skull —and perceived severe mental retardation. He cited the interior of the skull as support for this judgment: measuring the space behind the retreating forehead, the paleontologist determined to his satisfaction that there was not much room for the frontal portion of the brain, which was then thought (incorrectly) to be the center of higher intelligence. So in brainpower he ranked the fossil man somewhere between apes and modern men—but closer to the apes.

Boule wrote disparagingly of the "brutish appearance of this muscular and clumsy body, and of the heavy-jawed skull that declares the predominance of a purely vegetative or bestial kind over the functions of the mind. . . . What a contrast with the men of the next period, the men of the Cro-Magnon type, who had a more elegant body, a finer head, an upright and spacious brow, and who have left behind so much evidence of their material skill, their artistic and religious preoccupations and their abstract faculties —and who were the first to merit the glorious title of

Homo sapiens!" Boule was willing to grant the Neanderthals the honor of the genus Homo, but he relegated them to a separate, aberrant species that had died out long ago.

Marcellin Boule was a man of excellent reputation and formidable diligence—virtues that made his errors all the more serious. Between 1911 and 1913, he published his conclusions in three exhaustive tomes. Packed with detail and ringing with confidence, these monographs had tremendous influence on scientists and the public alike. Although a small minority of prehistorians stuck to their view that Neanderthals were perfectly respectable ancestors of modern man, practically everyone now felt that such a lineage had been scientifically proved impossible, since the Neanderthals were so thoroughly apish.

The sheer force of Boule's work was not the only reason for accepting it. Some circumstantial evidence pointed toward an evolutionary gap between the Neanderthals and Cro-Magnons, who were acknowledged ancestors of present-day humans. Even if the Neanderthals were not quite as debased as Boule supposed, they definitely looked different from the Cro-Magnons, and no one had ever come across a fossil that indicated an evolutionary transition between the Neanderthals and such a handsome modern man as Cro-Magnon. Without an intermediate fossil, it was only prudent to assume that the Cro-Magnons derived from stock that had been occupying Europe or some other part of the world during—or possibly before—the era of the Neanderthals.

Furthermore, archeologists felt that there was no cultural connection between the Cro-Magnon and Neanderthal peoples. The stone tools of the Cro-Magnons seemed markedly more sophisticated than the Neanderthal implements. And when archeologists dug down through successive layers in caves, they sometimes found toolless—"sterile"—layers between the Neanderthal deposits and the deposits left by Cro-Magnons, indicating that no one had occupied the cave for a time. The sterile layers were interpreted as proof that the Neanderthals had become extinct without ever having established a link with the Cro-Magnons.

During the decades after Boule's study, very little was said in support of the Neanderthals as human ancestors. His analysis not only won almost universal acceptance but also inspired some even less flattering views. For example, Elliot Smith, a noted anthropologist at University College, London, wrote in the 1920s of the "uncouth and repellent Neanderthal man" whose "nose is not sharply separated from the face, the two being merged in what in another animal would be called a snout." He further noted that Neanderthal man was not only marred by a "coarse face" and a "peculiarly ungraceful form" but probably had "a shaggy covering of hair over most of the body." Despite the fact that the Neanderthal hand was clearly human in formation, Smith claimed that it "lacked the delicacy and nicely balanced cooperation of thumb and fingers which is regarded as one of the most distinctive human characteristics."

Anthropology textbooks began to depict Neanderthals with the slumped, bent-knee posture that Boule had postulated. Standing this way, the creature's center of gravity was located in front of his center of support—and by all laws of physics he should have fallen flat on his face. Some textbook illustrators averted the danger by showing a Neanderthal taking a long stride forward; presumably he would have had

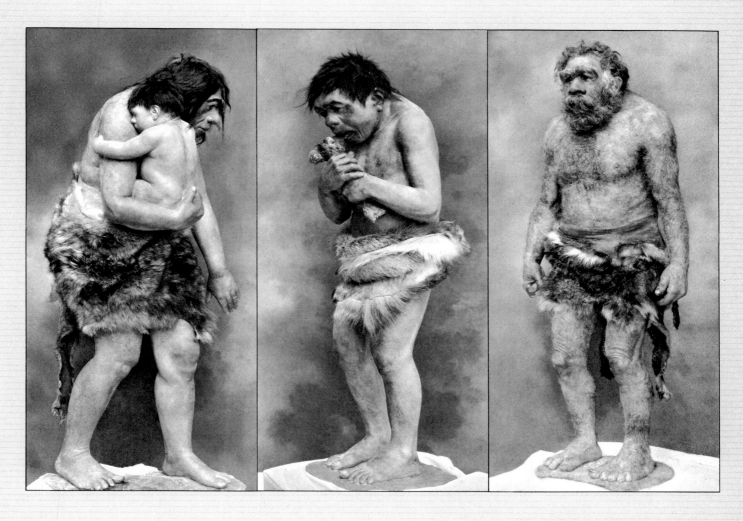

Typical of the misconceptions that have misled experts and laymen about Neanderthals are these diorama figures, a nursing mother and two tool-bearing men displayed in a Chicago museum for many decades. Their hunched shoulders, dangling arms and apelike posture are exaggerations at best. Most deceiving of all are their bovine expressions; real Neanderthals were people of considerable intelligence.

to keep walking to stay upright. And popular writers ... well, they could hardly be expected to exercise restraint. In a short story entitled *The Grisly Folk and Their War with Men,* H. G. Wells offered this portrait of a Neanderthal: "Hairy or grisly, with a big face like a mask, great brow ridges and no forehead, clutching an enormous flint and running like a baboon, with his head forward and not like a man with his head up, he must have been a fearsome creature for our forefathers to come upon." The Neanderthal vocabulary, according to Wells, consisted mainly of the word "Ugh." Predictably enough, the tale ended with the violent demise of these brutes.

Boule had depicted Neanderthals as creatures that might have had a hard time surviving, much less thriving, in the world. But if territorial range was any measure of success they seemed to have done quite well. As the years passed, Neanderthal fossils were found all over Europe, from Rumania and the Crimea in the east to the western lands of Spain and the Isle of Jersey. Still, as long as there was no evidence of them outside Europe, they could be written off as a localized evolutionary fluke. Prehistorians could thus safely claim that the main line of human evolution belonged elsewhere, in a still-unlocated Eden. (This problem-dodging tactic has been called the "over there" school of prehistory.)

But the beast-man would not stay put. In 1921 some laborers who were mining lead and zinc ore in Northern Rhodesia, thousands of miles from Europe, uncovered human bones that resembled Neanderthals. The fossil fragments came from a cave in a knoll called Broken Hill, which rose above plateau country just north of the Zambesi River. There were few clues to the actual date of the man, but the presence of stone tools and extinct animal bones indicated considerable age.

This fossil man had a low skull and receding forehead like the European Neanderthals. The ridges of bone over the eyes were more pronounced than any yet seen. But he also had a progressive trait: his limb bones were straighter and more slender than those of the European Neanderthals. (One other feature, interesting but not particularly significant, was the severe decay of the man's teeth. This is the earliest known case of tooth decay, perhaps caused by a lot of honey in his diet.)

The newly discovered fossil was named Rhodesian man. Where did he fit into human evolution? Some scholars, echoing Virchow, proclaimed that he was a modern-day mortal who was deformed by disease. A British expert, entrusted with the job of describing the bones for his fellow scientists, went to the opposite extreme. Following Boule's example, he declared that the formation of the pelvis "leaves no doubt that the gait of Rhodesian Man was simian, and that he walked with a stoop." He considered the creature "nearer to the Chimpanzee and Gorilla than was Neanderthal Man."

Most scientists, however, agreed that this man was the African version of the aberrant Neanderthal type. They began to wonder if some other members of the breed had lived in Asia. A positive answer was soon forthcoming. In 1931 fragments of 11 primitive individuals were dug from the banks of the Solo River on the island of Java, the Southeast Asian home of Pithecanthropus. The fossils, collectively named Solo man, were badly shattered, but there were enough fragments to suggest a kinship with the Neanderthals

—although the thickness of the skulls suggested an even lower evolutionary level. The hiatus between Java and Europe was filled in by another find in the desolate Alai Mountains of south-central Russia, about 78 miles from the fabled city of Samarkand. A cave in a cliff called Teshik-Tash (The Pitted Rock) yielded the fossilized remains of a boy who was clearly a Neanderthal.

During the early 1930s a joint Anglo-American expedition was looking for fossils in what is now Israel, then called Palestine. They struck fabulous pay-dirt in two caves on the slopes of Mount Carmel, overlooking the Mediterranean near Haifa. The first find, at Mugharet et-Tabun (Cave of the Oven), was a female skeleton, definitely Neanderthal but possessing a slightly higher than usual skull and a more vertical forehead. A second Mount Carmel site, Mugharet es-Skhul (Cave of the Kids), yielded remains of 10 individuals. Some resembled Neanderthals, others looked a bit more advanced and one approached the appearance of modern man. This last individual displayed a trace of the thick Neanderthal brow ridge, but the forehead was steeper, the jaw more delicate, the chin more pronounced and the shape of the cranium distinctly modern.

The total impression left by the Skhul people is that they occupied an evolutionary middle ground between the Neanderthals and modern man. But the assumption that all Neanderthals belonged to a dead-end species was, by now, so deeply entrenched that most experts could not believe the Mount Carmel specimens were direct ancestors of people living today. Some anthropologists concluded that the fossil men from Palestine were hybrids—products of intermarriage between true Neanderthals and true modern-type men who lived somewhere in the same area. The children of such a union could be expected to show a blend of primitive and modern traits. Scientists who favored this view also maintained, however, that such intermarriage may have been rare and need not have affected the main course of human evolution. One of the most famous of paleoanthropologists, the late Louis Leakey—discoverer of the Australopithecines—even suggested that any marriage between Neanderthals and modern-type men might well have produced sterile offspring, like a mule born of a horse-donkey mating.

All those who relegated Neanderthals to a side branch of human evolution believed (and some still do) that modern men existed somewhere on earth during the Neanderthal era. A few had even suggested that Homo sapiens existed millions of years ago. Most authorities, however, dated the origin of humans like ourselves to 200,000 or 300,000 years ago. The early true men supposedly waited in the wings all through the heyday of the Neanderthals, biding their time in an unknown land. Then, about 40,000 years ago, the true humans leaped into the evolutionary spotlight, either killing off the beast-men or allowing them to succumb to their own ineptitude.

But if modern man existed so long ago, where was he hiding? Generations of scholars have devoted their careers to a search for a very ancient but modern-looking ancestor. On several occasions, it seemed as though their search had been rewarded, but each time the fossils that appeared to represent a very old true man failed to fulfill their promise. For example, Marcellin Boule had advanced two fossils—Grimaldi man and Piltdown man—as proof of the great antiquity of modern man. But a recent analysis of the Grimaldi

How Different Faces Can Fit a Single Skull

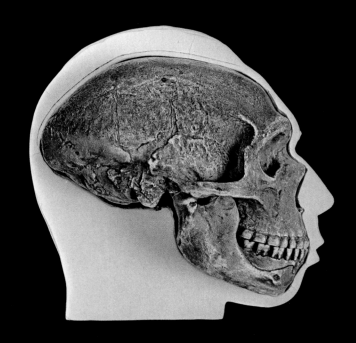

How could early reconstructions of Neanderthal man's appearance have been so wrong? And is today's accepted version of "the truth" indeed true?

Nobody knows the answers to these questions, but these two reconstructions, prepared especially for this book and shown here in full-face and profile views, show how widely divergent interpretations come about. Both of the heads start from the same Neanderthal skull, the so-called man from La Chapelle-aux-Saints, France, but end up looking strikingly different. The difference arises from the exercise of anatomically justifiable artistic license in reconstructing the soft tissue that once gave external shape to the head—but has long since disappeared because it does not fossilize as skull bones do.

In the version at top, the artist has supplied the skull with flesh and features that give Neanderthal a modern look: beetle-browed and heavy-jawed, but clearly a relative of today's man. The version at bottom applies 19th Century ideas of the nature of Neanderthal man to reconstruct the lost, soft tissues of the head. With more hair, a thicker neck, a fleshier mouth and a wider, flatter nose, the same skull presents Neanderthal as a creature more ape than man.

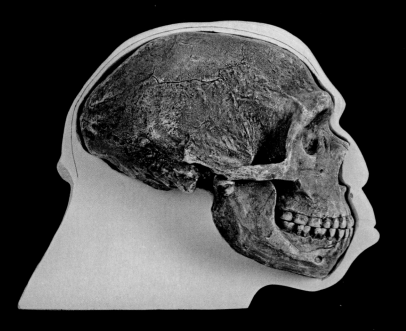

site, in Italy, has shown that the fossil is actually of rather recent vintage, postdating the Neanderthals. The explanation for Piltdown man is simpler—and considerably more embarrassing to those who had embraced him. This fossil, found in a gravel pit in England and announced to the world in 1912, had a perfectly modern skull and an apelike jaw. The extraordinary amalgam of traits was not the handiwork of nature, however. Piltdown man was a fake. Some hoaxer had stained a modern skull to make it look old, added the jaw of an orangutan, thrown in a few ancient animal bones collected from around the world—and deceived practically everybody. Finally in the early 1950s, the hoax was exposed by chemical tests clearly showing that the skull and jaw were completely unrelated.

The fossil that came closest to proving the early origin of true man was discovered in some gravel deposits in the Thames Valley, near the village of Swanscombe, England. Only the skullcap was found. The forehead, face, jaw and lower skeleton were gone. Yet many anthropologists felt that the skull fragments possessed a shape and size that surely indicated a modern type of human, probably a female. And this time there was no doubt about the authenticity and the great age of the find. Geological evidence indicated that the woman of Swanscombe lived about 250,000 years ago.

There was an obvious difficulty in considering the Swanscombe fossil a full-fledged Sapiens. What could possibly explain the fact that the Neanderthals had lived in Europe *after* people of the progressive Swanscombe race, who presumably would want the region all to themselves, and would have been able to defeat the more primitive people? One explana-

tion offered in the 1950s postulated that the Neanderthals were a chill-resistant breed who arose in eastern Asia and migrated to Europe during a bitterly cold glacial period; meanwhile, the progressive Swanscombe people had the good sense to get out of Europe and go to Africa or tropical Asia. Later, when the weather improved, they snatched back their old territory from the Neanderthals. Most authorities, however, found these logistics far too complicated. They preferred the view that Neanderthals and true men had lived side by side in Europe, perhaps occupying different sorts of environments so that there was no competition between them.

In any case, as long as Swanscombe was accepted as very old in years and modern in development, the Neanderthals had to be interpreted as an aberrant offshoot of evolution. But was the Swanscombe fossil really so progressive? The skull fragments looked quite similar to another equally ancient skull dug up near Steinheim, Germany. This German specimen came with an upper jaw and forehead, both quite primitive in appearance. If the skulls were related, as they seemed to be, the Swanscombe fossil could not be considered a modern type of human but in fact a very early Neanderthal. The debate wavered back and forth until 1964, when two Cambridge scientists enlisted the help of a computer to ascertain the status of the Swanscombe woman.

They took 17 different measurements of the Swanscombe and Steinheim skulls; then, for purposes of comparison, they measured various Neanderthal skulls as well as some modern ones. The computer was programed to work out "distance functions" —numerical statements of evolutionary relationships. It whirred through its calculations and cranked out the opinion that the Swanscombe fossil was no more modern than the Steinheim skull. Instead of being precociously sapient, both were about as primitive as would be expected from their ancient date. Thus, what seemed to be evidence for the presence of true men far back in time was again discounted.

The computer examination of the Swanscombe fossil is one of many helpful new approaches to prehistory. During the 19th Century and much of the 20th, scientists had the unenviable task of making sense out of a mere handful of fossils. Dates were uncertain or sometimes impossible even to guess at. A lack of information about human variability often caused experts to make too much of one trait or another. It is easy to go wrong about fossils, exaggerating, for example, the significance of a particular curve at the back of a skull or incorrectly reconstructing features when parts are missing. Today these errors and inadequacies are being remedied. Statistical mathematics is used to reduce subjectivity in analyses of fossils or artifacts. The discovery of various sorts of radioactive isotopes has enabled archeologists to establish ancient dates far more accurately than used to be possible. And a great many other specialized skills have been developed to improve the focus and perspective on distant time. Anthropologists are still fallible, of course, but less so than ever before.

Improvements in techniques have proved particularly fruitful for the study of Neanderthals. New fossils have been identified in many parts of the world—China, Central and North Africa, Iraq, Czechoslovakia, Hungary, Greece and elsewhere —bringing the total number of Neanderthal individuals today to more than 100. And with the discovery of new and better evidence has come a drastic change in the appraisal of Neanderthals.

The old prejudices began to evaporate in 1955, when several scientists suggested that the slumped posture described by Boule might be in error, since even young children learning to walk, or apes standing on their hind legs, are fully upright. But the major turnabout came in 1957, when two anatomists, William Straus of The Johns Hopkins University and A.J.E. Cave of St. Bartholomew's Hospital Medical College in London, took a second, closer look at the fossil from La Chapelle-aux-Saints that had provided the basis for Boule's contentions. The fossil was supposed to be typical. However, Straus and Cave discovered that this particular Neanderthal had suffered from a severe case of arthritis, which affected the formation of the vertebrae and the jaw. Boule, as a skilled paleontologist, should have detected the deformation of the bone joints indicating the disease. Straus and Cave also spotted many other inexplicable mistakes in Boule's reconstruction. The Neanderthal foot, for example, was definitely not a "prehensile organ," as Boule had said. The neck vertebrae did not resemble those of a chimpanzee nor was the pelvis apelike in structure, as claimed. All in all, Straus and Cave found Neanderthal man to be quite human indeed. They wrote: "If he could be reincarnated and placed in a New York subway—provided that he were bathed, shaved and dressed in modern clothing—it is doubtful whether he would attract any more attention than some of its other denizens."

By removing the taint of apishness that had been associated with Neanderthals for so long, the Straus-Cave study effectively revived the Neanderthals' candidacy as possible ancestors of modern men. It is still true, of course, that the fossil from La Chapelle-aux-Saints does not look much like a Cro-Magnon or most humans of today, and many anthropologists continue to deny an ancestral relationship. However, the Neanderthals uncovered at Mount Carmel definitely cannot be dismissed from human lineage on the basis of looks, for they possess a blend of Neanderthal and modern traits. The theory that explains their intermediate appearance as the result of mixed Neanderthal and Cro-Magnon parentage is doubtful since there is no evidence that both types of humankind were living in the world during the same period of time. The Middle Eastern fossils therefore serve to establish a solid evolutionary link between Neanderthals and modern men.

Even so, many questions remain. Did Neanderthals all over the world make the evolutionary transition to modernity, or did only a few select populations accomplish it? What evolutionary forces propelled the change? And what can account for the apparent revolution in toolmaking techniques that occurred shortly after 40,000 B.C. or for the sterile layers that often separate the Neanderthal and Cro-Magnon periods of cave occupancy?

Someday the questions will be answered, but it now seems unlikely that the outcome will ever demote the Neanderthals from the mainstream of human evolution. Science has accordingly adjusted its view—and its classification—of Neanderthal. With the overthrow of the Bouleian vision, and the clarified status of the Swanscombe fossil, the Neanderthals have been granted the taxonomic title of *Homo sapiens*. On the end of this title is tacked the subspecies term of *neanderthalensis* (or *rhodesiensis* or *soloensis*), denoting some difference from fully modern man—now technically known as *Homo sapiens sapiens*. But that first appellation of *sapiens* places the Neanderthals squarely in the human fold. We stand on their burly shoulders.

Techniques of a Master Hunter

Scouting for game, a Neanderthal hunter kneels to gauge the size of a cave bear from the tracks it left in a glacial sand deposit.

As Neanderthal man grew in numbers he spread outward from the regions occupied by his predecessor, Homo erectus, into areas that were often colder and less benign, such as the windswept tundra of northern Europe. Forced to rely more on meat for nourishment when rigorous winters and deep snows made edible plants and berries scarce, Neanderthal hunted far less haphazardly than Homo erectus, in larger bands and with studied intent: from the evidence left behind at his kill sites, and scattered around his hearths, he knew a great deal about animal behavior, and he planned his hunts accordingly.

Naturally, Neanderthal man's preference was for big game because it provided more nourishment for more people. And his world during those times of icy climates was, by today's standard, a big-game hunter's paradise. Among the fossilized bones found buried with the blackened remains of his campfires are those of reindeer, horses, ibex, elephants, elks, bears, bison and such now-extinct creatures as the woolly rhinoceros and mammoth and the cattlelike aurochs—many of them larger and presumably more pugnacious than their modern counterparts *(pages 115-121).*

Armed with clubs, Neanderthal men interrupt their hunt for big game to pursue hares for the Stone Age equivalent of a light lunch. They are about to hurl their weapons at a skittering animal to daze it; then they will dash up to wring its neck. Though snow dusts the tundra landscape, the low-growing foliage is the green of late spring and the hares have begun to acquire their brownish summer coats. Small game such as this was a regular item of the Neanderthal diet —often contributed by the women and children.

Hapless horses, driven to the brink of a precipice by hunters brandishing torches, plunge to their doom. This successful kill needed the cooperation of many men, some to head the horses —smaller than those of today—toward the cliff, others below to finish off the fallen animals with clubs and spears.

Breaking from cover, a hunter hurls his spear into a reindeer. To catch such quick and alert animals, Neanderthal had to ambush them, stampede them into bogs or, following the strategy of wolves, watch for signs of weakness in one of the herd, cut it out from the group, tire it and then close in.

Turning on its assailants, a beleaguered woolly
rhinoceros attempts to fight off a band of Neanderthal
hunters. With stones and shouts, they have driven the
rhino to the rocky bank of a shallow river, intending
to trap it in the bottom and then move in with wooden
spears for the kill. But the beast has attacked its
attackers and has gored one (left). The wounded man's
companions, their anger roused, plunge their spears
into the rhino's chest, aiming for the heart.

Jumping up from his hiding place behind a boulder, a Neanderthal hunter swings a bola—strips of rawhide weighted with stones—and aims it at the legs of a fleet-footed Stone Age zebra. The bola will wrap itself around the animal's legs, slowing the zebra down enough for other hunters to catch up and slaughter it with their spears and clubs. The bola is still used today; Argentinian gauchos employ similar stone-weighted ropes to check and capture cattle.

Chapter Two: Men of the Ice Ages

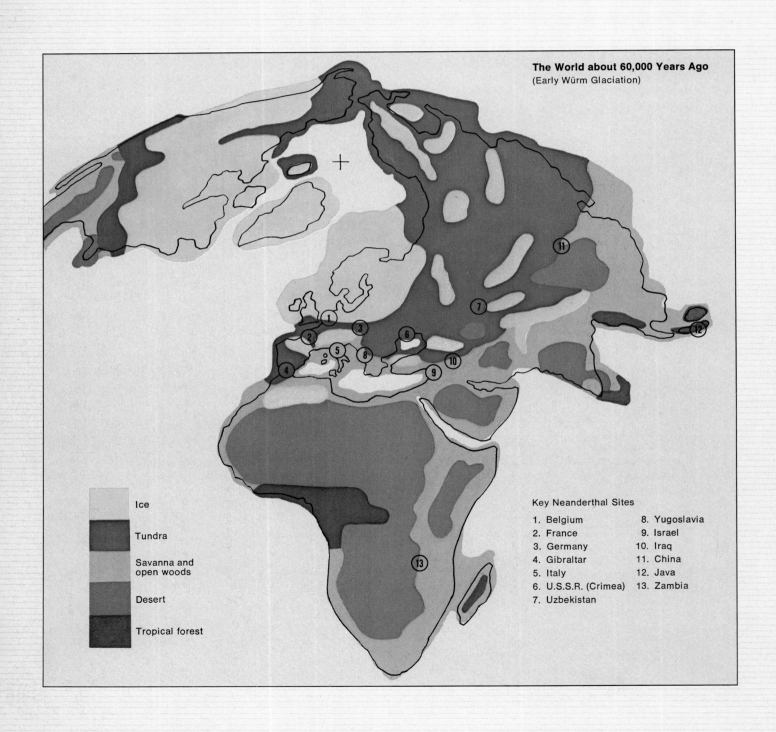

The World about 60,000 Years Ago
(Early Würm Glaciation)

Ice

Tundra

Savanna and
open woods

Desert

Tropical forest

Key Neanderthal Sites

1. Belgium
2. France
3. Germany
4. Gibraltar
5. Italy
6. U.S.S.R. (Crimea)
7. Uzbekistan
8. Yugoslavia
9. Israel
10. Iraq
11. China
12. Java
13. Zambia

Neanderthal man was the last of the archaic men, not the first. He stood on shoulders burlier than his own. Behind him stretched five million years of slow evolution, during which *Australopithecus,* the not-quite-human offspring of apes, became the first species of true man, *Homo erectus,* and Erectus begat the second species, *Homo sapiens.* That second species lives on today. The earliest Sapiens evolved into a long line of human varieties and subvarieties culminating in Neanderthal and finally in modern man. Neanderthal thus climaxes a major stage of development within the *Homo sapiens* species—nothing followed him but modern man, who is a member of the same species.

Neanderthal appeared on earth about 100,000 years ago. Yet by that time other varieties of Homo sapiens had been around for another 200,000 years or so. Only a few fossils of these pre-Neanderthal Homo sapiens types—grouped by paleoanthropologists under the catch-all "early Homo sapiens"—have been found, but substantial numbers of stone tools have turned up, and it is possible to re-create with some assurance the lives these ancient people led. An understanding of their progress is essential, for the story of Neanderthal, like any proper biography, must begin with an account of his immediate ancestors. Imagine one moment of perfect well-being, 250,000

Though the large land masses of the ice-age world were roughly equivalent to those of today (superimposed in outline in this artist's rendering), their climates—and hence their vegetation—were not. At the beginning of the Würm glaciation, during Neanderthal times, ice sheets (color key) expanded and tundra spread south. Temperate and savanna woodlands encroached upon once-warmer areas, including parts of the Mediterranean that are now underwater, while deserts and patches of intermittent tropical forest covered hot regions.

years ago. A man is standing immobile in an upland meadow in England, visibly pleased by the smell of warm meat in the air as his companions butcher a newborn fawn that they have killed. His task is to watch for predators or scavengers while the other men dismember the fawn with their heavy, sharp-edged tools of stone. Even though the meadow appears empty, he never relaxes his vigilance, for a lion could be crouching in the grass or a bear might be watching from the nearby woods. But the possibility of danger only sharpens his awareness of the sights and sounds of his bountiful land.

The rolling hills that stretch away into the distance are covered with oak and elm, now in full leaf. After a mild winter, spring has brought such warmth to England that the man is comfortable without clothes. He can hear hippos celebrating the season with deep bellows as they splash in the willow-lined river a mile away. The crack of a branch signals the presence of a bear or perhaps some ponderous elephant or rhinoceros browsing among the trees.

Standing there in the sun, with a slender wooden spear in one hand, this man does not appear especially powerful, although he is five and a half feet tall, well muscled and clearly capable of speed afoot. His head might be suggestive of meager intelligence, for the brow slants back from an outthrust face, and his skull looks low and pinched-in at the sides. But he has a larger brain than his ancestor, the man known as Homo erectus, who carried the torch of human evolution for more than a million years. This man's brain size, in fact, is nearing the modern level; hence he can be considered a very early member of the modern human species, Homo sapiens.

The English hunter belongs to a group of about 30

individuals. They inhabit a territory so large that a trip from border to border would take several days —yet this expanse of land is just enough to keep them supplied with meat throughout the season; in a smaller territory they would have to hunt so intensively that the population of grazing animals would be depleted. At the edges of this range live other small bands of humans who speak a similar dialect and are closely related to the English hunter's group through intermarriage. Beyond these immediate neighbors are other bands—less closely related, speaking alien languages—and, beyond them, still others. The earth and man's role in it were greater than the hunter could possibly imagine.

Two hundred and fifty thousand years ago the population of humans in the world was probably fewer than 10 million—about the same as that of modern Tokyo. But this unimpressive total is deceptive, for humankind occupied far more of the earth's surface than any other single species. The English hunter lived at the northwestern outpost of man's geographical range. To the east, beyond the horizon, similar small bands of a half-dozen or a dozen families were camped in a broad valley, today covered by the waters of the English Channel. Still farther east and south, hunting-and-gathering groups were spread all across the face of Europe.

Most of Europe was then woodland, frequently interrupted by lush glades or meadows, with temperatures so warm that water buffalo thrived in central Germany and monkeys chattered in rain forests along the Mediterranean. The greater portion of Asia was less hospitable, and human bands avoided the heartland of that continent because of the harsh winters and dry, blistering summers. But men were scattered around the entire southern perimeter of Asia, from the Middle East to Java and northward into central China. In all probability the most densely populated continent was Africa. This sprawling land mass may have contained a population larger than the rest of the world put together.

The sort of lands settled by these various peoples reveals much about their ability to deal with nature. They almost invariably lived in grassy or partially wooded country. There was a very good reason for this preference: these regions supported the herds of grazing animals that provided much of the meat in the human diet. Wherever herd animals were lacking, men also stayed away. The unoccupied areas included deserts, rain forests and the dense coniferous woods of the north—a very substantial portion of the earth's surface. A few herbivorous animal species did exist in the forests of the north and south, but mostly they wandered alone or in small groups, for the scantiness of forage and the difficulty of moving through thickly packed trees made herd life impractical. The finding and killing of animals that were solitary grazers was so difficult at this stage of human development that men simply could not prosper in these regions.

Another environment that resisted human invasion was the tundra of the far north. Here, obtaining meat was not the problem. Enormous herds of reindeer, bison and other large, easy-to-kill animals found ready forage in the tundra country—there were plenty of mosses, lichens, grasses and shrubs, and few trees to get in the way. However, men could not yet cope with the extreme cold of the region. Early Homo sapiens consequently stuck to the same lands that had supported his Homo erectus ancestors

—the savannas and open thorn forests of the tropics, and the grasslands and airy deciduous woodlands found in the temperate latitudes.

It is remarkable that anthropologists have been able to learn so much about the world of these early Sapiens, considering their distance in time and the scantiness of evidence from the period. Many materials that were essential to early men are highly perishable. Foods, hides, sinews, wood, plant fibers and even bone last no time at all except under the rarest conditions. The few scraps of organic materials that have survived often seem more tantalizing than informative. Take, for example, a sharpened piece of yew wood, thought to be 300,000 years old, found at Clacton-on-Sea in England (the wood was preserved because the site was waterlogged). It may have come from a spear, for the tip had been dried by holding it over flames, rendering it hard enough to penetrate the hides of animals. However, this hardened wood point may have served some entirely different purpose, such as digging up edible roots.

Yet such seemingly ambiguous clues can be interpreted. In a case like that of the yew fragment, common sense helps. Men were certainly using both spears and digging sticks well before this artifact was made. But it seems that a man would be more likely to take the trouble to harden a spear point than a digging implement. Similarly, there is every reason to believe that men who lived in cool climates wore some sort of clothing many hundreds of thousands of years ago, even though their garments —undoubtedly of animal skins—have not endured. It also seems certain that shelters were regularly constructed and, in fact, the impressions of postholes at one site on the coast of France prove that men knew how to make simple huts of branches and animal hides even back in Homo erectus' times.

A posthole here, a piece of wood there, a bit of sharpened bone, an occasional hearth—these are the whispered hints of human achievement in remote times. The heroes and heroines of the tale, however, have so far proved to be very elusive. Only two fossils exist to suggest that an early form of Sapiens existed some 250,000 years ago—low-crowned, thick-boned skulls found at Swanscombe, England, and Steinheim, Germany.

However, some clues to the past are more readily available. Geological deposits laid down during any given period can reveal a good deal about climate, including the temperature and the amount of precipitation. Pollen found in the deposits can be identified under a microscope, indicating exactly what kinds of trees, grass or other vegetation prevailed. Most important of all for the study of prehistory are stone tools, which are virtually indestructible. Wherever early men lived, they left stone implements, often in fantastic abundance. One cave in Lebanon, occupied by men for an estimated 50,000 years, has yielded more than a million flints.

As a source of information about early man, stone tools are intriguing. They tell nothing about some of the most interesting aspects of ancient life—family relationships, tribal organization, what people said or thought, or how they looked. In a sense, an archeologist digging down through geological layers is in the position of a man on the moon listening to radio broadcasts from Earth with a weak receiver: out of all the thousands of signals of music and talk that are being transmitted from stations around the

Early Tools
Hacked from Stone

By the time the Neanderthals appeared on the scene, men had been toolmakers for well over a million years and had developed not only several kinds of tools, but traditional techniques for their manufacture. One of the oldest and most widespread of these techniques, called the Acheulean, was taken up and used by many Neanderthal peoples, although others preferred a later technique called the Levallois *(pages 56-57)*.

In the Acheulean tradition the tool was sculpted from a stone by chipping away at it until the rock was the desired shape. Three typical Acheulean flint tools are shown here in full view and profile, and almost exact size.

Thick, rough-edged and irregular, the 400,000-year-old Acheulean hand ax at left is nevertheless a versatile and efficient implement. Its point and two cutting edges were used to chop, pierce and scrape.

Tapering to a slender tip, this
200,000-year-old hand ax
was shaped with a stone hammer.
Then its edges were refined
with a hammer of hard wood
or bone, whose more resilient
blows yielded smaller chips.

The long, almost straight right-
hand edge of the 200,000-year-
old side scraper at right is
the working edge. Chipped
depressions in its top, visible in
the full view, provide grips for
the thumb and fingers.

globe, he picks up only one signal loud and clear—in this case, implements of stone. Yet much can be learned from a single station. First of all, whenever an archeologist finds tools, he knows that men once lived there. Comparison of tools from one site with contemporaneous tools from another site may suggest cultural contacts between ancient populations. And comparison of tools in successive layers can help trace the cultural progress and the intelligence levels of the early men who left them.

Stone tools reveal that, although the men living 250,000 years ago were intelligent enough to deserve the title of Sapiens, they had a great deal in common with their less advanced Erectus forebears. Their tools were made according to a style that had originally appeared hundreds of thousands of years earlier. This style is named the Acheulean tradition after the French site of Saint Acheul, near Amiens, where such tools were first discovered. The Acheulean tradition included a characteristic implement called a hand ax—a flattish oval or pear-shaped tool with cutting edges running along each side of its five- or six-inch length (pages 42-43). The tool would have been suitable for many purposes—piercing hide, butchering animals, chopping or scraping wood, and many other everyday tasks. Hand axes might have been wedged into thick wooden clubs to form a "compound" implement like a modern hatchet or ax. But it is more likely that they were always hand held (perhaps a piece of animal hide was wrapped around the butt to protect the user's hand).

The double-edged hand ax was supplemented by flakes of stone, which were sometimes notched or given a saw-toothed edge, for finer work on carcasses or wood. Some people showed a preference for flakes instead of the larger hand axes; others rounded out their tool kits with heavy cleavers for hacking apart the joints of larger animals. However, the basic outlines of the Acheulean tradition were followed by people in all parts of the world except the Far East, where a somewhat cruder tradition of single-edged implements held sway.

While the worldwide uniformity of stonecrafting indicates a paucity of inventiveness, the hand ax was being gradually improved in small ways. As men learned to chip the raw materials of flint or quartzite with soft hammers of bone, wood or antlers instead of with hard rock hammers, they were able to produce hand axes that had sharper, more regular cutting edges (page 78). In the difficult world of early men, a better cutting edge on the all-purpose hand ax would have been an enormous asset.

In the deposits left by the early Sapiens people, there are other stone tools that point to growing perspicacity and a willingness to experiment. At about this time, some particularly ingenious hunters initiated a major new technique for making flake tools. Instead of simply banging away at a large nodule of flint to produce flakes—an inherently wasteful procedure—they developed a very sophisticated and efficient manufacturing process. First, a flint nodule was chipped around the side and on the top; then this prepared core was rapped at a particular point on its side. The blow resulted in a flake of predetermined size and shape, with long sharp cutting edges. This Levallois technique, as it is called (page 56), represents a remarkable insight into the potential of stone, for no tool is visible until the very end of the process. In the making of a hand ax, the tool gradually and reassuringly takes shape; but a Levallois flake springs full-blown out of a core of flint that in no way resembles a tool, like a butterfly emerging from the totally dissimilar tissues of a caterpillar. The Levallois method seems to have originated about 200,000 years ago in southern Africa and spread outward from there, although it may have been independently discovered in several places.

When all the different kinds of evidence are put together—tools, a few fossils, a bit of organic material, along with pollen and various geological clues to climate—the people of that remote time start to come alive. They were sturdy men, with quite modern bodies but rather apelike faces and brains of nearly modern size. They were master hunters who could cope with all but the harshest environments. Culturally, they were clinging to the traditions of the past, but they were slowly inventing their way toward a tighter, more secure hold over nature.

Theirs was a fairly hospitable world. But it was destined to change—abruptly in geological terms—to become as inhospitable an environment as the human race has ever known. Somehow Homo sapiens lived through these upheavals and emerged strengthened by his ordeal, more adaptable, more skillful and more intelligent than before.

About 200,000 years ago, the weather began to grow colder. Glades and meadows in the deciduous woodlands of Europe broadened at an imperceptible rate—the tangled rain forests along the Mediterranean began to wither; and the expanses of spruce and fir in eastern Europe slowly yielded to the encroachment of the steppe. Perhaps the elders of the European bands had a note of dread in their voices as they recalled years when the wind did not bite so sharply and snow never fell. But since the band's way

of life was nomadic to begin with, it was easy enough to follow wherever the herd animals led. Groups that formerly had had no pressing need for fire, clothing or artificial shelter now had to take a lesson in cold-weather survival techniques from northern peoples, who had been practicing such arts ever since the days of Homo erectus.

Snow was falling in the mountain ranges of the world—more snow than could melt during the summer. Year by year it piled up, filling deep valleys and compacting itself into ice. The stupendous weight of the ice caused its lower layers to behave like very thick putty, sliding outward from the valleys as the ever-accumulating snow pressed down from above. Inching through the mountain ranges, the great fingers of ice plucked boulders from cliffsides and used them like a giant's scouring powder to grind the once-green land down to bedrock. In the summer, torrents of meltwater carried the debris of sand and rock dust out in front of the advancing glaciers, where it was later picked up by winds and blown across the continents in great yellowish-brown clouds. And still the snow continued to fall, until in some places the ice sheets grew more than a mile thick, burying the mountains and causing the very crust of the earth to sag under the load. At their fullest extent, the glaciers covered more than 30 per cent of the world's land surface, compared to a mere 10 per cent now. Europe was especially hard hit. The surrounding ocean and seas offered a limitless source of moisture for snow, which fed separate glaciers bulldozing outward from the Alps and the Scandinavian ranges to cover vast stretches of the continent.

This glacial age, known as the Riss, was one of the worst climatic traumas in the five-billion-year his-

How Spreading Ice Challenged Ancient Men

During the many thousands of years when early Homo sapiens peoples were evolving toward the Neanderthal type, their world was again and again chilled and constricted by the advance of glaciers. In Europe, particularly, ancient men were caught between two separate floods of ice. While huge sheets pushed out from the north, down from the Alps flowed mountain glaciers like the one at right—frozen rivers with many-branched tributaries that filled valleys and blocked passes.

The combination of the continental ice sheets and the mountain glaciers squeezed the ancient men of Europe into relatively small patches of tundra, largely because the glaciers were too treacherous or rough-surfaced to clamber across. The roughness comes about as a result of the ice's twisting movements. As a glacier is forced to flow over or around an obstacle—as, for example, when it must turn corners like those at far right and far left in the picture—the creeping movement tugs diagonally at the crust, wrinkling it and forming crevasses, some of which are hidden by a thin crust of snow. The corrugations seen at bottom center may be as much as 100 feet deep and 10 feet wide. Although many mountain glaciers were fairly narrow—the branch visible at bottom in this picture is about a half mile wide—their great thicknesses and perilous surfaces made them impassable to animals and men alike.

A typical mountain glacier, this survivor of the ice ages of the past has four tributaries entering fro

the top and sides of the picture to create a wrinkled river of ice about a mile across; the crunching ice flows down the slope toward the bottom.

tory of the earth. Although similar cold spasms had occurred before, during the days of Homo erectus, the Riss was the first to try the endurance of Homo sapiens. He was to survive 75,000 years of bitter cold, interspersed with mild spells, before the earth warmed up again—for a time.

Many experts believe that a necessary precondition for glaciers is the slow building of plateaus and mountain ranges. It has been estimated that one age of mountain-building raised the average height of the world's land surface by an average of more than 1,500 feet. Such an increase in elevation would lower the temperature on the surface by an average of three degrees—and probably much more in the highest places. The temperature drop would certainly increase the probability of glacier formation, but it does not explain why cold and warm periods alternated the way they did.

A number of explanations have been proposed for these variations in the earth's climate. One theory holds that volcanoes from time to time spewed tremendous amounts of fine dust into the atmosphere, blocking off some of the warming radiation of the sun. Scientists have observed a worldwide lowering of temperature at times of major volcanic eruptions, but the cooling is very slight and lasts no longer than 15 years, thus making volcanoes an unlikely trigger for glaciation. Yet other kinds of dust could have had greater effect. Some astronomers have speculated that clouds of cosmic dust have periodically passed between the sun and earth, diminishing radiation over long periods of time. Since such cosmic dust clouds have not been seen in action, this idea remains an interesting guess.

There is another astronomical explanation for ice ages that seems more credible. Variations in the angle of the earth's axis of rotation and in its orbit around the sun change the amount of solar heat striking the planet, and these alterations, calculations show, would have produced four long periods of lowered temperature during the past three quarters of a million years. No one knows whether these temperature changes were sufficient to produce glaciation, but they undoubtedly had a contributing effect. Finally, the sun itself may have had something to do with glaciers. The amount of heat and light radiated by the sun varies in a cycle whose period averages 11 years; the radiation rises when sunspots and giant flares erupt on the sun, falls to a slightly lower level as these solar storms abate—and then repeats the pattern. Some astronomers believe that the radiation of the sun may undergo long-term fluctuations akin to this short-term sunspot cycle.

Whatever the cause of the climate changes, the impact was enormous. During these cold periods, the wind system of the world was disrupted. Rainfall increased in some places and diminished in others. Patterns of vegetation were greatly altered. And many animal species died out or evolved new, cold-adapted forms, such as the cave bear and woolly rhinoceros (pages 34-35).

During some particularly severe phases of the Riss glaciation, England, which had been so pleasant when the earliest Homo sapiens lived there, became so bitterly cold that midsummer temperatures were often below the freezing point. The temperate woodlands of central and western Europe were transformed into tundra or steppe. As far south as the shores of the Mediterranean, trees gradually died and were eventually replaced by grassland.

The picture in Africa is less clear. In some places, reduced temperatures apparently were accompanied by greater rainfall, allowing trees or grass to grow on formerly barren parts of the Sahara and Kalahari deserts. At the same time, changing wind patterns had a drying effect on the dense Congo rain forest, causing it to give way to open woodland or grassland. Thus, while Europe was becoming less habitable, Africa was becoming more so, favoring an expansion of men throughout much of that continent.

The land resources available to men during the Riss ice age were also augmented by a worldwide lowering of sea levels. So much water became locked up in the huge ice sheets that the level of the oceans dropped by as much as 500 feet, exposing large areas of the continental shelves—the shallow subsea plains that reach outward from the continental margins, in some places for hundreds of miles, before dropping off steeply to the ocean floor far below. The baring of formerly submerged land gave hunters access to millions of square miles of new territory, and there is no doubt that they took advantage of this dividend of the ice age. Each year, bands wandered farther into newly dried land, and they may even have established camps close to thundering waterfalls where rivers cascaded over the edge of the continental shelves and into the oceans below.

During the 75,000-year paroxysm of the Riss glaciation, inhabitants of northerly latitudes suffered hardships that were unknown during the balmy period of the earliest Sapiens peoples, and these hardships may have had a stimulating influence on human intelligence. Some experts believe that the great rise in intelligence that had already occurred during the era of Homo erectus was due to man's expansion out of the tropics and into cool regions where ingenuity and flexibility of behavior were more necessary for survival: Erectus pioneers had to learn to use fire, invent clothes and shelter, and adjust to complex seasonal schedules for the availability of animal and vegetable food. The Riss, with its widespread ecological disruptions, would have tested—and perhaps boosted—intelligence in the same way.

Early Sapiens peoples maintained a foothold in Europe even during the worst of times. Stone tools offer indirect proof of their continuing presence there, but until recently human fossils from this period were lacking. Then, in 1971, a French husband-and-wife team of archeologists, Henry and Marie-Antoinette de Lumley of the University of Marseilles, turned up evidence of one beleaguered European band living in a cave in the foothills of the Pyrenees during the early part of the Riss, about 200,000 years ago. Along with a number of stone tools—mostly flakes—the De Lumleys found the crushed skull of a man about 20 years old. This hunter had a forward-jutting face, a thick ridge of bone over the eyes, a slanting forehead and a brain case somewhat smaller than the modern average. Two jaws found at the same site are massive and seem well suited to chewing coarse food. The skull and jaws match up well with the Swanscombe and Steinheim fragments, giving us quite a detailed picture of men intermediate between Homo erectus and Neanderthal.

From the mouth of their spacious cave, these people looked out on a land that was bleak but abounding in game. Straggly willows and bushes clung to the edges of a river running through a gorge directly below the cave. Here, panthers lay in wait for wild horses, goats, oxen and other animals that came to drink. Beyond the gorge, a treeless steppe slid away to the horizon, and the hunters would have seen herds of elephants, reindeer and rhinoceros moving slowly about under the leaden sky. The big animals, along with an occasional rabbit or rodent, provided more than enough food to support the band. Yet life was extremely rugged. It took real hardihood to venture out into the freezing wind and endure the stinging dust and sand that blew across the plain. And far worse times must quickly have followed, for these people were forced to leave for some better place —as is indicated by the absence of tools in the layers above. There is evidence that, for a time, the climate there took on truly arctic bitterness.

Recently at Lazaret in southern France the De Lumleys made another spectacular find—remnants of shelters that had been constructed *inside* a cave. These simple shelters, dating to the latter part of the Riss, about 150,000 years ago, were tents, probably consisting of animal hides stretched over a framework of branches and anchored by stones around the perimeter (page 73). Perhaps the hunters who occupied the cave from time to time set up the tents to give families some privacy or to keep off water that dripped from the ceiling. But the weather must have been a consideration, too. The entrances of the tents were oriented away from the cave mouth, suggesting that winds blew cold and hard even at this spot close to the Mediterranean.

Another remarkable clue to the growing complexity and subtlety of human behavior turned up at Lazaret. The De Lumleys found a wolf skull located just inside the portal of every tent. The similar placement of each skull in each location makes clear that these remains were not bones tossed away as gar-

A Fossilized Face from the Distant Past

The first full-faced view of Neanderthal man's immediate predecessor (*far right*) appeared in 1971, when a skull with its delicate facial structure still intact was dug up in a cave near Tautavel on the French side of the Pyrenees. The discoverers of the fossil, anthropologists Henry and Marie-Antoinette de Lumley of the University of Marseilles, believe it to be that of a young male, probably a member of a nomadic hunting band living in the cave about 200,000 years ago—some 100,000 years after the Homo sapiens species replaced Homo erectus, and 100,000 years before Neanderthal appeared.

Like Homo erectus fossils, the Tautavel skull has a forehead sloping back sharply from bony eyebrow ridges, but the groove between the ridges and the brow is less pronounced. The face juts forward—not as much as Erectus' but more than Neanderthal's; the jaws and teeth are also larger than Neanderthal's. The brain size, while not easy to estimate because the skull is crushed on one side, is apparently larger than in Homo erectus and smaller than in Neanderthal. From these comparisons it seems clear that Tautavel man filled a place midway in the evolutionary gap between the first men and the Neanderthals.

Unworn surfaces on molars show they belonged to a youth.

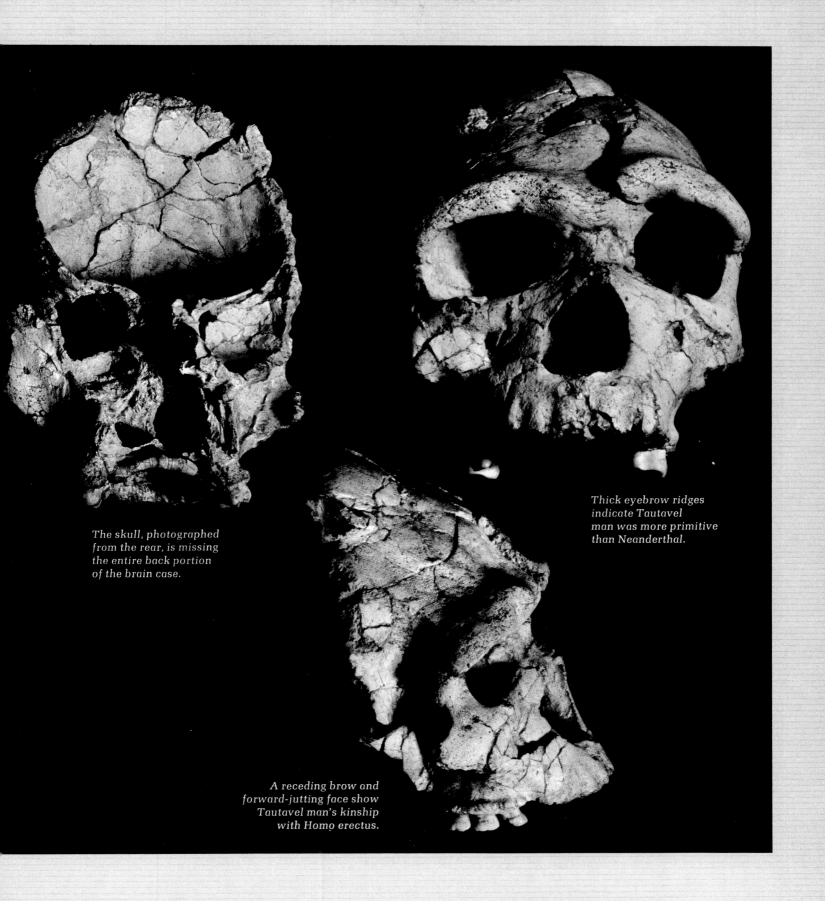

The skull, photographed from the rear, is missing the entire back portion of the brain case.

Thick eyebrow ridges indicate Tautavel man was more primitive than Neanderthal.

A receding brow and forward-jutting face show Tautavel man's kinship with Homo erectus.

bage. They undoubtedly signified something. But exactly what is still a mystery. One possibility is that whenever the hunters departed to pursue their nomadic activities elsewhere, they left wolf heads behind as supernatural guardians of their homes.

Around 125,000 years ago, the long climatic agony of the Riss tapered off and another period of warmth began. It was destined to last about 50,000 years. Glaciers shrank back into their mountain fastnesses; the seas rose; and northern latitudes all across the world once again became an inviting place for humans. A few intriguing fossils are dated to this period, and they testify to continuing modernization of Homo sapiens. From a cave near the town of Fontéchevade in southwestern France come skull fragments, perhaps 110,000 years old, that seem more advanced than the Riss-age man from the Pyrenees.

By the time the warm period following the Riss glaciation reached its midpoint, about 100,000 years ago, Homo sapiens had evolved into a true Neanderthal, and the transitional period from the early Sapiens people was ended. There are at least two fossils to prove the arrival of Neanderthal, one from a quarry near Ehringsdorf, Germany, the other from a gravel pit on the banks of the Tiber River in Italy. These European Neanderthals gradually evolved from the genetic stock of people like the man from the Pyrenees and the later, more modern Fontéchevade Homo sapiens. The Neanderthals were not very different from their predecessors. The human jaw was still massive and chinless; the face was still outthrust; and the skull was still low, with a sloping brow. But the volume of their brain cases was now completely up to the present-day size. When anthropologists use the term Neanderthal as a description of a certain evolutionary status, they are referring essentially to a type of man who had a modern-sized brain that is packaged in an archaic-looking skull —long and low, with a big face.

It is difficult to evaluate this full-sized brain. Some theorists feel that it does not necessarily signal the attainment of the modern level of intelligence. Noting that brain size ordinarily increases with body weight, they suggest that if the Neanderthals were a few pounds heavier than the early Sapiens, the added body bulk might account for the growth in cranial capacity—a matter of a few hundred cubic centimeters at most. In other words, Neanderthals were not necessarily smarter than their ancestors, just heftier. But this argument seems doubtful, for most students of evolution believe there is a direct relationship between brain size and intelligence. Admittedly, the relationship is hard to define. Measuring intelligence by brain volume is a bit like trying to assess a computer's powers by weighing it.

If Neanderthals are given the benefit of the doubt and rated—on the basis of brain volume—as equals of modern man in raw intelligence, another problem arises. Why did the expansion of the brain cease about 100,000 years ago, since intelligence is of such obvious value to humanity? Why would the brain stop growing larger and presumably better?

Ernst Mayr, a Harvard biologist, has offered an answer. He speculates that intelligence increased with remarkable rapidity prior to the Neanderthal stage of evolution because the most intelligent males became leaders of their bands and were permitted to have several wives. More wives meant more children. The leaders would therefore contribute a disproportionate share of genes to later generations. Mayr suggests that this intelligence-boosting process came to an end about 100,000 years ago, when, in his view, the size of hunting-gathering groups grew so large that the more intelligent leaders would have no particular fertility advantage. That is, their genetic bequeathal of exceptional intelligence to later generations would make up only a small and rather insignificant part of the genetic endowment of the group, rather than a major share.

C. Loring Brace, a physical anthropologist at the University of Michigan, prefers another explanation. In his view, human culture in Neanderthal times reached a point at which almost all members of a band had a fairly adequate chance of survival so long as they could master the traditions of their band. If language were then sufficiently developed—a supposition disputed by some authorities—and if intelligence were sufficiently high so that the least brainy members of a band could be educated in the necessary survival techniques, brilliance would confer no evolutionary advantage. Some individuals were especially innovative, of course, but their ideas would be communicated to everyone, and the whole band would benefit from any advance. Thus, according to Brace, the raw intelligence of humanity as a whole became stabilized, although men continued to increase their knowledge about the world.

These are heady speculations, and most anthropologists prefer a more down-to-earth approach. They feel that the only fair way of assessing the powers of the Neanderthal brain is to find out how such early men dealt with the world after they appeared. These scientists tune in on stone technologies—the one loud, clear signal transmitted across the expanse of time—and detect evidence of quickening intelligence everywhere. The old Acheulean tradition of hand axes still persisted, but it was becoming ever more varied. The double-edged hand axes now came in many sizes and shapes, often so symmetrical and painstakingly trimmed that esthetic impulses seem to have guided their makers. When a man made a small hand ax for roughing out spears or a notched flake to strip the bark off the shaft of the spear, he made it right, taking care to shape the implement for maximum efficiency at its intended work.

In toolmaking, Europe seems to have been a center of innovation. Since it is bounded by seas on three sides, the early Sapiens bands living there had had no easy avenue of escape to warmer regions during the Riss glaciation, and even the Neanderthals were occasionally isolated for certain periods later, when cold snaps occurred during the warm era following the Riss. Disruptive environmental changes in Europe would have been a sharper spur to experimentation than the more even climates of Africa or Asia.

About 75,000 years ago, that spur was applied to Neanderthal man with renewed force as, once again, glaciers began to grow. This most recent glacial age, known as the Würm, was not severe at first. The Würm initially brought snowy winters and cool rainy summers. Nevertheless, open grassland spread, and formerly wooded portions of Germany and northern France were transformed into tundra or a forest-tundra mixture where open areas of moss and lichens alternated with stands of trees.

During preceding ice ages, the early Sapiens bands had generally pulled back from such uncongenial lands. Now the Neanderthals stayed—at least in the summertime—subsisting off the herds of reindeer, woolly rhinos and mammoths. They must have been first-rate hunters, for tundra country offered little vegetable food to tide them over lean days. No doubt the death toll was high on this northernmost frontier, and bands remained small and probably not very healthy. Away from the frigid verge of the ice sheets, populations were more dense.

The tenacity of the Neanderthals in the north and the thriving state of those in milder areas must have been due, at least in part, to the advances in stonecrafting that took place during the early Würm. The Neanderthals invented a new stoneworking method that brought about a permanent ascendancy of the versatile tools made from flakes over those made by shaping a heavy core. Fine flake tools had long been made by the Levallois technique, which involved knocking two or three finished flakes off a preshaped hunk of stone, and this technique continued to be used in some places. But the new method was far more productive: many Neanderthals now trimmed a nodule of stone around the edges to make a disk-shaped core; then, aiming hammer blows toward the center of the disk, they repeatedly rapped at its edges, knocking off flake after flake until the core was almost entirely used up. Finally, the unfinished flakes were further trimmed to give them the edges needed for work on wood, carcasses or hides.

The great virtue of this new disk-core method was that it allowed men to produce large numbers of usable flakes with little effort. And since flakes can easily be retouched to give them a particular shape or edge, the new technique ushered in a portentous era of specialization in tools. Neanderthal tool kits were far more versatile than those of earlier men. Francois Bordes, a French archeologist who is the world's fore-

most expert on Neanderthal stonecrafting, lists more than 60 distinct types of cutting, scraping, piercing and gouging tools. No single band of Neanderthals used all these implements, but the kit of a given band nonetheless contained a great many special-purpose tools—saw-toothed implements, stone knives with one blunt edge so that pressure could be more firmly applied, and many other types. Possibly some pointed flakes were attached to the ends of spears by wedging them into the wood or tying them on with thongs. With such an arsenal of tools, men could exploit the world of nature as never before.

Everywhere north of the Sahara and eastward as far as China, these retouched flakes became the preeminent tools. The tools made within this broad area are collectively called Mousterian (after the French site of Le Moustier, where flake tools were first found, back in the 1860s). South of the Sahara, two distinct new styles appeared. One, called the Fauresmith tradition, was really a highly evolved version of the Acheulean, including small hand axes, a variety of scraping tools and narrow flake knives. The Fauresmith kit was used by people living in the same grassy regions favored by earlier Acheulean hunters. The other new style, called Sangoan, was characterized by a type of long, narrow, heavy tool—which may have served as a combination machete and stabbing weapon—as well as some hand axes and small scrapers. This style, too, represented a major departure from the Acheulean tradition. Although the tools seem crude in appearance, they were well suited to cutting and shaping wood.

From 75,000 to about 40,000 years ago, the Neanderthals conquered a whole series of habitats that had repulsed their ancestors. The European Neanderthals accepted the challenge of tundra country and won. Some of their African relatives, equipped with Sangoan tools, penetrated the forests of the Congo basin and hacked paths through the dense vegetation that replaced much of the grassland during rainy times. Other Neanderthals were spreading across the vast plains of the western U.S.S.R., and still others ventured into the rugged mountain chains of southern Asia and out the other side, thereby opening up the Asian heartland to human existence. And, moving along routes where waterholes were not too far apart, some Neanderthals entered regions that were almost as arid as true desert.

These conquests were not achieved by dramatic migrations. No band was suicidal enough to pack up its scanty possessions and walk 100 miles into an area that its members knew nothing about. Instead, the expansion into new habitats was accomplished by a process anthropologists call budding. A few individuals would split away from a prospering group and found their own autonomous band in nearby territory where the food resources were somewhat marginal. If they could make a go of it, their population would grow, and later generations might split off into even more marginal areas.

Specialization was the order of the day. The northern Mousterians were the supreme clothesmakers of the world, as indicated by their numerous scraping tools, which could be used in preparing hides. The Sangoans may have been the most skilled woodcrafters, and perhaps they learned to construct animal traps to catch forest creatures that, wandering singly through the woods, were much more elusive than herds grazing on a savanna. People were also beginning to focus on the hunting of certain kinds of an-

imals—a remarkable shift from the catch-as-catch-can approach that had characterized hunting since earliest times. The proof of their specialization can be seen in one particular European tool kit, known as Denticulate Mousterian because it emphasizes flakes with toothed or notched edges. Denticulate Mousterian tools are always found in association with the bones of wild horses. Apparently, the people who made these tools had so thoroughly mastered the knack of killing horses that they ignored all the other grazing animals around them and spent their days in quest of the kind of meat they liked best.

Where certain key resources were lacking, the Neanderthals tried to overcome the difficulty. On the treeless plains of central Europe, they began to experiment with bone tools that could take the place of wood. Water was another resource in short supply over large parts of the earth's surface, and humans had always been forced to stay within walking distance of streams, rivers, lakes or springs. But the Neanderthals invaded some very dry lands by utilizing water vessels—not pottery bowls but shells. Recently, in the sun-baked Negev region of Israel, ostrich egg shells turned up along with Mousterian tools. The large egg shells would have made fine canteens, enabling a band to survive a journey across the parched hills from one waterhole to another.

The sheer abundance of Mousterian tools alone is enough to affirm that the Neanderthals greatly outstripped their predecessors in their ability to garner a living from nature. There is no doubt that they greatly enlarged the dominion of man. The conquests of new territories that occurred during the time of the Neanderthals represent the greatest expansion of humankind since Homo erectus had wandered out

Precision Tools of a Gifted People

Many toolmaking methods were used by Neanderthal man, but the one he favored most is called Mousterian; it produced the points and scrapers shown here. Unlike earlier tools, which were essentially shaped stones (*pages 42-43*), these Mousterian tools were made from stone flakes. Each flake was struck off a stone "core," which itself was trimmed in advance —so that the face of the flake was in effect predetermined. The basic flaking technique, called Levallois, had been in existence some 100,000 years before the refinements were developed by Mousterian toolmakers. In their skilled hands the method worked so well one core could provide a maximum number of flakes that could then be tailored to the Neanderthals' needs.

Turtle-back core and point

Prism core and scraper

Rough-shaped into a prism, a very early Mousterian core (above) supplied flakes for a series of tools. One of them could be the side scraper shown in two views at right, whose flat face seems to match the core's indented surface.

Disk core and two tools

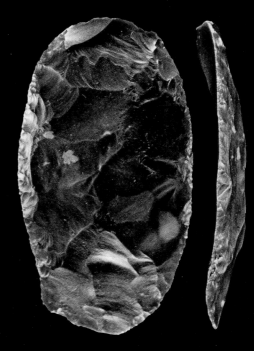

Trimmed in a shape that is reminiscent of a turtle's shell, the Mousterian core at left was flaked across its flat-bottom face to provide materials for tools like the point shown below in full view and profile.

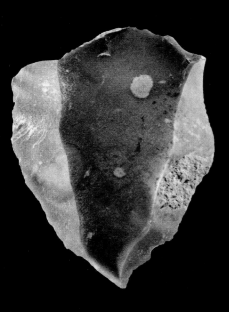

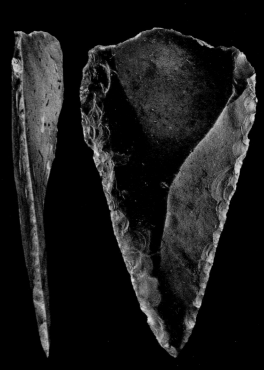

Little remains of the much-flaked core above except a circular piece: refinements in the initial shaping of the core, and in the way it was struck, permitted the toolmaker to flake the core until it was almost all used up. Such technical mastery could then turn the flakes into implements like the double-edged scraper, at right above, and the thin-bladed point, at right, both shown in full view and profile.

of the tropics and into cool latitudes hundreds of thousands of years earlier.

Yet the failures of the Neanderthals also are revealing. They never reached the heart of the tropical rain forests, and they probably did not make much of a dent on the thick forests of the far north. Colonization of these regions called for more sophisticated survival techniques than they could devise.

What about the New World? Access to the incredible riches of the Americas was theoretically possible during the early part of the Würm ice age. Glaciers again were locking up moisture and lowering the sea level. As a result, a broad flat land bridge emerged between Siberia and Alaska. This was inviting tundra country, with a wealth of big game. From Alaska south to the rest of the Americas, the road was closed at times by the glaciers of western Canada and the Rocky Mountains, but during some millennia passage was possible. However, the difficulties of getting to the land bridge were formidable. Eastern Siberia is a hilly region sectioned by mountain chains. Even today, its climate is almost intolerable, with some of the lowest temperatures ever recorded. During the Würm, conditions must have been still worse.

A few doughty Neanderthal bands seem to have established a foothold in the southern part of Siberia, which then consisted of grassland and partially wooded tundra, instead of the dense unbroken forest that now mantles the region. Gazing north and east, they would have seen endless hills reaching into the unknown. Plentiful supplies of meat beckoned —horse and bison, and woolly mammoths with great curved tusks that could scrape at the crust of snow to get at the forage beneath. The temptation to follow the herds must have been great. And if the hunters had suspected that a bridge to incomparable gamelands lay beyond the horizon, they might well have attempted the journey. For these were certainly not men of small spirit. Burly in form, hardened by constant crisis, inured to the prospect of dying by violence, they were born and bred to adventure. But these people also knew instinctively that, even now, they were trespassing on death's own ground: one bad winter storm could snuff them out. And so the Neanderthals did not reach America. Until men developed better clothing, more efficient weapons and warmer sorts of shelter, the New World would remain empty of humans.

From the vantage of the present, it is tempting to criticize the Neanderthals for missing this magnificent opportunity, or for failing to reach Australia, or for turning back from the densest parts of jungles and coniferous forests. And in many other ways, they did not measure up to the men who came after them. The Neanderthals never really grasped the potential of bone as a material for tools; they did not know about the art of sewing, which would require bone needles; they did not know how to weave baskets or make pottery; and their stone tools were inferior to those of the people who lived after them. But the Neanderthals could be regarded from another viewpoint. If, by some miracle, the early Sapiens hunter who lived in a balmy England 250,000 years ago could have been transported to a Neanderthal camp in glacier-gripped Europe during the Würm glaciation, he would surely have been overcome with amazement and admiration for what his species had accomplished. He would have seen men and women making a good living in an environment that would have overwhelmed him.

Space Age Methods for Solving Stone Age Mysteries

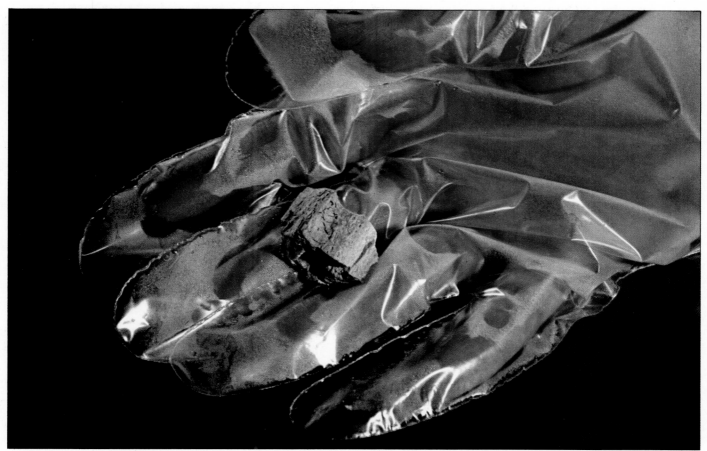

A scientist's sterile glove protects a bit of Neanderthal-era bone from contamination as he prepares it for a chemical dating test.

Less than an ounce of bone held in a scientist's gloved hand: from such fragmentary vestiges of ancient man as this, the mysteries surrounding the Neanderthals are at last being dispelled. For in recent years scientists have developed a remarkable array of improved laboratory tools to turn time backward and see the world as it existed in the days of the distant past.

The bit of bone shown in the picture, for example, will be dated by a recently developed technique that reveals the passage of time by measuring chemical changes in the molecules making up proteins. An even smaller sliver of bone, scrutinized with a device that, in effect, color-codes crystal structure, will tell something about the kind of life that was led by the owner of the bone. And soil from which bone is unearthed can, from its sediment composition, indicate the climate of the time when the bone was part of a living creature. By such methods, a few fragile relics suffice to re-create Neanderthal days.

Reading an Ancient Skeleton's Protein Clock

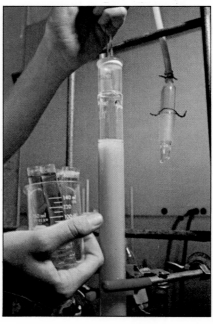

To date a bone, a sample is dissolved in hydrochloric acid (below), and passed through chemicals to trap amino acids (bottom). Acids are then washed off trapping chemicals and combined with a "carrier" that enables right-handed molecules to be separated from left-handed ones (right).

To tell the age of the objects they unearth, archeologists rely on a number of dating methods that are all basically types of atomic clocks. The "ticks" that make these clocks keep time are naturally-occurring, uniform changes in the structure of certain atoms—a different kind of change for each clock. If the rate of the change —the length of the tick—is known, a measurement of the amount of change can reveal how much time has passed since the change began within the atoms of the fossil.

Simple enough, but not that simple for studying Neanderthal man. For the most generally used atomic clocks measure time from the present back to about 40,000 years ago, and from about 500,000 years ago to the earth's beginning. Between these times is a dating gap, and in that gap is the time of the Neanderthals. Only recently have two clocks been perfected to time the gap and dispel some of the mysteries surrounding the Neanderthals. One type can date the remains of Neanderthal men and animals. The other can verify the age of Neanderthal tools and flint.

The dating method illustrated at the right gauges the age of ancient skeletal remains with a protein clock. It capitalizes on a process, called racemization, within amino acids, the substances that form the basic building blocks of the protein making up all living organisms. There are 20 different amino acids, but all have at least this much in common: their molecular architecture is "left-handed" —that is, the atoms of each molecule are arranged asymmetrically, in a direction that appears left-handed because of the way the structure is analyzed. But when an organism dies, the molecules of its amino acids begin to realign rightward. This slow change into the mirror-image "right-handed" molecules is racemization.

In 1972 and 1973, an organic chemist at the University of California's Scripps Institution of Oceanography, Jeffrey Bada (opposite page, at left), published his calculations of the rates at which several different amino acids undergo racemization at moderate temperature—one changes its form at a rate so that half is altered in 110,000 years, easily covering the 40,000-to-100,000-years-ago span of Neanderthal man's existence on earth.

To date an ancient bone, Bada reduces a sample to its amino acid constituents and adds a compound that alters the acids' right-handed and left-handed molecules into substances that can be separated in a series of complex steps. By comparing the relative quantities of right-handed and left-handed acids with their known rate of racemization, Bada can tell how much time has passed since the death of the creature whose bone he is testing. So the dating gap is filled, at least for once-living finds.

Jeffrey Bada fills a syringe to inject treated amino acids into a separator. Right-handed forms trickle down the separator column (center) faster, coming out two to four minutes before left-handed ones. Further treatment colors both in turn, and color intensity indicates the quantity of each acid.

Bada's forefinger points to a peak (dashed line), plotted from color measurements, representing a quantity of left-handed amino acid; to its left, a lower peak represents right-handed acid. The closer the peak heights, the longer since the organism died. The top graph, bone of known age, is a check.

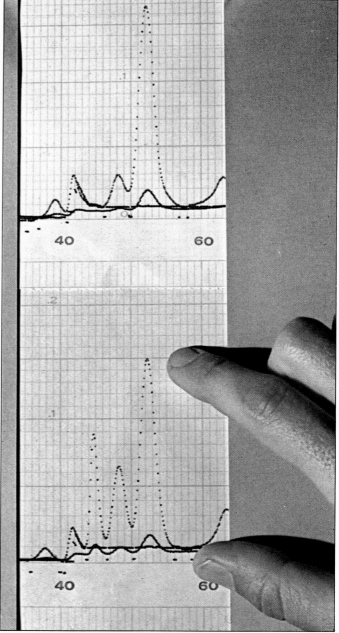

How Shifting Atoms Set a Date for a Long-cold Fire

The protein clock (*preceding pages*) fills the dating gap in the record of early man—but only if the remains being studied were once alive. Shown on these pages is a method for dating many kinds of inanimate objects, including stones that have been heated in ancient hearths.

The stone-dating method depends on thermoluminescence, the production of light by shifts of atomic particles when certain minerals are heated. The heat (in a Neanderthal campfire, for instance) causes the particles to move toward the centers of the atoms, releasing energy in the form of light. When the stone cools, the particles shift once again away from the atomic centers. This gradual shifting outward is the clock mechanism. The archeologist testing the stone subjects it to heat again. The amount of light released tells him how long the particles had been shifting outward, and thus how long it has been since the stone previously was heated by some caveman's fire.

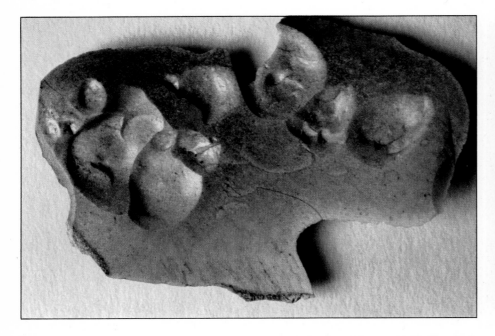

This bit of flint stone, half an inch across, may have been chipped off a rock when a Neanderthal man was sharpening a tool beside his campfire. The chip, which apparently dropped into the flames, then underwent an atomic change brought about by the heat of the fire: natural movements of the particles within some mineral atoms were reversed, only to start up again after the flint had cooled.

To gauge the age of a stone, only a tiny polished sliver—shown on the tip of a technician's finger—is needed. This sliver is placed on an electric heating element in a special measuring instrument (picture at right), which not only raises the temperature to the required level but also detects the amount of light released by the heated stone and translates that into a signal to make the graph opposite.

The peaked curve on the sensor's graph
indicates the stone's light emission
—and thus the atomic shifting in its
atoms since the flint was heated
before, dating the ancient fire. The
lower curve graphs incandescent glow.

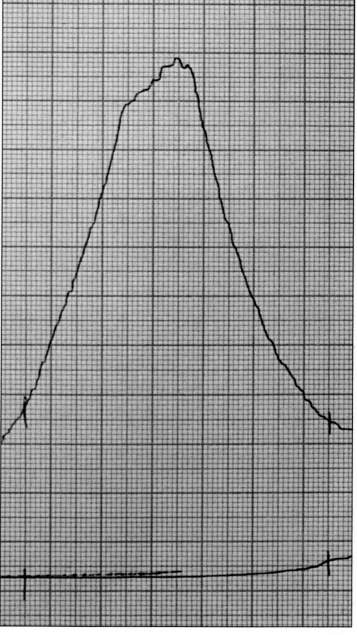

Life Styles Revealed in Buttressed Bone

Having found and dated a bone from Neanderthal times, scientists are beginning to analyze its structure for clues to the way its owner lived, since they suspect that the arrangement of crystals within bones depends in part on physical activity. This inner structure is revealed by examining a slice of bone with a microscope and polarizing filters, which regulate the planes of vibration of light waves and create color patterns—the color depending on crystal alignment. When bones of modern wild animals, which lead active lives, are examined this way, they display a murky magenta hue—an indication of a dense, random crystal structure of great strength. Quite different are the bones of modern man and domesticated animals, which lead more sedentary lives. They appear turquoise and yellow, indicating a lighter structure of crystals in an open, buttressed alignment. Neanderthal bones (right), magenta like those of wild animals, suggest dense structure and constant exertion.

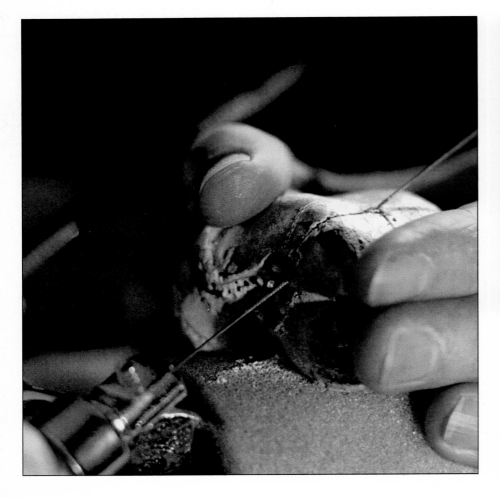

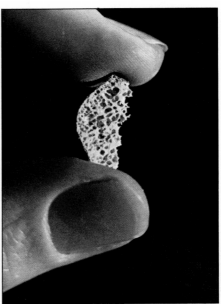

Working with a jeweler's saw (left), a mineralogist slices a wedge from a 50,000-year-old Neanderthal foot bone unearthed in Iraq. The wedge (above), about half an inch high, is ground paper thin and polished until nearly transparent. It is then scrutinized under polarized light to reveal colors indicating a dense, random crystal structure (right), stronger than the more open crystal formation indicated for modern man's bone (far right).

Photographed with the mineralogist's polarizing equipment, the Neanderthal bone segment exhibits a densely packed crystal structure, indicated by a magenta tinge. Physiologists associate this strong type of bone with relatively great physical activity.

A modern human bone has an open latticework that appears blue and yellow when viewed with a polarizing microscope. Efficient geometric alignment of the crystals helps buttress this lighter bone, but it is still weaker than the heavy Neanderthal type.

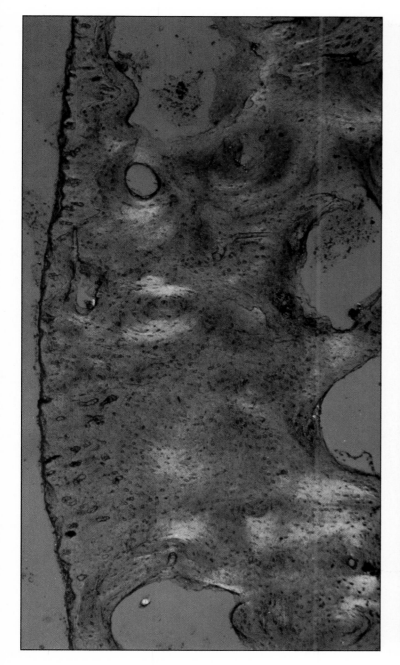

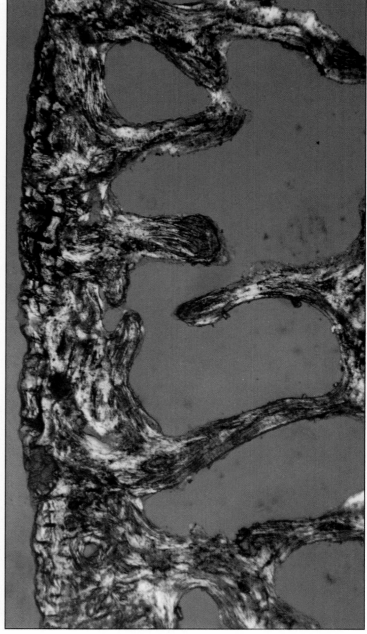

The Soil's Report on Weather of Prehistoric Times

The earth in which Neanderthal bones are found can be as revealing as the bones themselves. For in its sediments is a record of the climate that formed the Neanderthal environment.

A typical excavation is a site called Mugharet et-Tabun on the slopes of Mount Carmel in Israel. Neanderthals lived in caves there for tens of thousands of years. The deepest layer of sediment, about 100,000 years old, consists of fine sand *(opposite page, left)*. Because the sand is loose rather than densely laid down, geologists know that it was wind-blown. But because the grains are so irregularly shaped, they must have been carried only a fairly short distance on gentle winds; grains spun along for great distances, or in sandstorms, become evenly rounded. The conclusion is that the sea was probably about as far from the caves as it is now, about two miles. The climate, then as now, was probably warm and dry. The Neanderthal inhabitants would not have needed much clothing.

But layers of sediment formed in succeeding centuries tell a different story. Those from 50,000 years ago contain little sand but bear traces of water-dissolved bone residues. If the bone dissolved, the environment must have been wet. Presumably great mud flats then stretched out before Mount Carmel, and the Neanderthals who stood there bundled themselves in hides as they gazed on a damp world.

Earth from a Neanderthal cave site in Israel, Mugharet et-Tabun, is prepared for analysis in a geologist's laboratory. A geologist holds a vacuum bell jar over a beaker containing sediments soaking in resin; when air is pumped out, the resin saturates the sediment pores. The next step is to bake the sediment sample for several hours. Permeated with the resin, it becomes hard enough to slice and polish for microscopic examination.

A clod of sediment from a prehistoric site, saturated with resin and baked hard, is sliced on this high-speed, water-cooled blade. Each slice—about .00003 inch thick—is ground and polished until it is completely transparent. Then the geologist studies these very thin cross-sections under a microscope. By identifying components such as sand, silt and clay in the sample (right), he can often deduce ancient environments.

The sediment from the lowest level at Tabun, about 100,000 years old, has a loose consistency and light weight, indicating dry breezes carried it; water-borne sand has grains of varying sizes. Jagged shapes suggest storms did not churn and polish the sand.

Sediment believed 50,000 years old is marked by a diagonal trail of chalky calcium phosphate remains of bone, possibly that of Neanderthals buried at the site. The fact that the bone residue had been dissolved indicates that Tabun was wetter at the time.

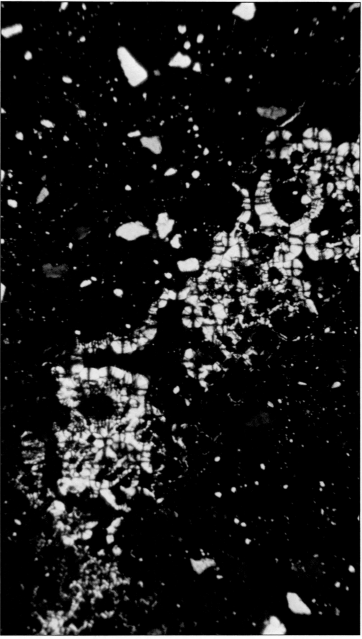

Using Electricity to Probe for Fossils

Before any laboratory can analyze the remains of Neanderthal man to learn about his environment and habits, archeologists have to find the materials to test by digging down into cave floors—and often their excavations turn out to be dry holes. Now one anthropologist, Steve Kopper of Long Island University in Greenvale, New York, has devised a way to assess a cave's archeological possibilities before a shovel is turned.

Kopper's test technique, which is known as electrical resistivity surveying, is not a brand-new invention. Geologists have been using it for many years to locate minerals and ground water. But its application to cave archeology is an innovation.

What Kopper does is implant four or more probes in the ground and pass a current between them. Wires connect the probes to a meter on which Kopper is able to read the amount of electrical resistance that the current meets at various depths in the ground. The resistance reading at each depth is then compared with similar readings on layers of known age in other excavations in the same general area. Layers of the same age will provide much the same resistance readings. In this way, Kopper can quickly survey a group of neighboring caves, comparing resistance levels to spot fresh sites that resemble existing, fossil-rich excavations—and perhaps find others that contain even older levels.

In a limestone cave, anthropologist Steve Kopper reads a meter connected to probes between which a current is sent. In this way he can measure the electrical resistance of underlying layers of earth, a clue to their age.

Chapter Three: Daily Life 60,000 Years Ago

The scene is Germany; the year, 60,000 B.C. Winter reigns here in the forested belt just south of the open tundra. The birch and willow and alder trees have long since dropped their autumn foliage. A carpet of brown and golden leaves lies buried under snow. All growth has shut down for the season, although the evergreen spruce and pines keep a semblance of life, in stolid contrast to the skeletal appearance of their deciduous cousins. Every few moments, one of the conifers shudders and spills its burden of snow to the ground with a soft thump. A breath of wind soughs in the pine needles, sets brittle willow branches chattering and sends little whirlpools of ice crystals spinning away in the lee of trees. Apart from such small motions and sounds, this seems to be a world bereft of activity. The snow-bearing stratocumulus clouds that hung over the land during November and December have departed for the moment. Now the sky is a bowl of blue, streaked on high by gauzy cirrus clouds.

But the stillness and silence of the world are deceptive. Under the protective blanket of snow, small rodents race along crisscrossing tunnels in search of seeds. Partridge, bundled in thick fluffs of feathers, hide in the bushes. White hares dance lightly among the trees, pausing to nibble bark. At the slightest hint of danger, they freeze, becoming virtually invisible against the background of snow. Death is never far

Mealtime in a Neanderthal cave is not without a small degree of refinement—the use of stone knives to cut roasted meat. Here a hungry hunter clamps a chunk between his front teeth and slices off a mouthful. In the process, Neanderthal man sometimes scratched his tooth enamel with the rough-edged knife—and thus gave scientists yet another clue to the kind of man he was. Because of the angle of the scratches, archeologists can tell that Neanderthal man was right-handed.

away. Hawks glide overhead on silent wings, eager to swoop down and crush a furry skull with scimitar talons. Foxes creep through the underbrush, competing for meat with the bigger, stronger lynxes.

Many larger animals inhabit this region as well. Mammoths and rhinos have moved south from the open tundra to winter in the partially forested zone where the trees offer some shelter against the piercing winds blowing off the glaciers. Herds of reindeer, bison and shaggy horses are also scattered across the land. They forage in bare, wind-swept meadows or scrape away the soft snow among the trees to get at the withered stems of grass beneath. Many of them browse on the branches of trees and shrubs. The large herbivorous animals are as vigilant as any hare, for packs of wolves prowl the forest-tundra. And there is a two-legged creature, as terrifying as any wolf, who hunts here too.

Every species of animal seems to avoid one particular locale, where a spring-fed stream slices between two hills and debouches into a long lake. The crust of ice on this stream is broken in several spots. Up the slope of one of the hills a wall of animal hides is stretched over a framework of branches. From an opening above this wall, smoke curls into the air. Behind the skins is a cave, its entrance facing south, away from the direction of the arctic winds. This is the winter home of a Neanderthal band.

Inside the cave the Neanderthals are hard to see at first, although the morning sun is up in the sky. The hides stretched across the opening cut off much of the sunlight, and only a single fire is burning within, close to the mouth of the cave. The air is damp and tainted by excrement and unwashed bodies, but still the tang of flaming pine boughs dominates.

Breakfast is about to begin. One of the women kneels down by the fire and brushes the coals aside to expose a hearth of flat stones beneath. These stones are now extremely hot and will serve as a griddle. She selects several hunks of meat from a nearby pile and tosses them on the stones. A hunter who likes his meat almost raw snatches up a piece after it has cooked less than a minute. Gripping one end of the meat between his teeth and the fingers of one hand, he cuts it in two with a sharp stone flake, then gobbles both pieces down, clinging ashes and all.

Even the minor actions of cutting and chewing bespeak the great strength of the man. He has the broad shoulders and barrel chest of a weight lifter. His large jaw, worked by bulging muscles, is a powerful and efficient lever that masticates the still bloody meat in no time at all.

Having breakfasted, the hunter is ready to begin the day in earnest. The five other men who live in the cave are beginning to stir too. Using long strips of hide as thongs, they tie a second layer of animal hides over the skins they have worn night and day throughout the winter. All of the men have stocky, muscular builds and the double wrapping of reindeer and elk furs gives them a bearlike appearance.

A tally of the cave's inhabitants reveals a curious male-female distinction: there are more men than women. One of the hunters apparently lacks a wife. The obvious explanation would be the death of a woman or a coincidental scarcity of marriageable females. However, among the dozen children still sleeping on their beds of animal furs, the boys outnumber the girls. The anomaly is not accidental. This northern band lives mainly on a meat diet, since vegetable food is scarce here. Hence, male hunters are more important suppliers of food than female gatherers. When excess females are born, they threaten the future survival of the band, and they must be eliminated by infanticide. But male infants are sometimes killed, too, in order to hold the size of the band within the limits of available food resources. The band of 23 needs almost 500 pounds of lean meat each week to stay in good health. Seldom is there enough to fill the communal "refrigerator"—a meat-storage pit dug in the ground outside the cave, lined with stones and covered with a heavy stone slab to keep bears, wolves and foxes from plundering the treasure within.

The men, after warming their hands above the fire, grasp their wooden spears and clubs and plunge into the cold. One of the five grown women of the band is preparing a hide for clothing. With a stone flake, she scrapes away the decaying tissue on the inner side of the pelt. After it has been fully cleaned, the hide will be slowly dried near the fire and then smoked to render it partially waterproof and resistant to shrinkage. Another woman takes some nuts from a pile in the back of the cave, cracks them open and begins to pound them into an edible powder.

At times like this, when meat is running short, the band—and especially the children—will have to rely heavily on stockpiles of nuts, bulbs, roots and seeds that were gathered during the months before the snows came. Some of these gathered foods are strictly starvation fare. For instance, the inner bark of willow trees can be eaten after much pounding with a stone, although no human seems to enjoy such a meal. But there are delicacies too: one storage pit outdoors holds a supply of frozen berries.

After breakfast, the children leave the cave to play

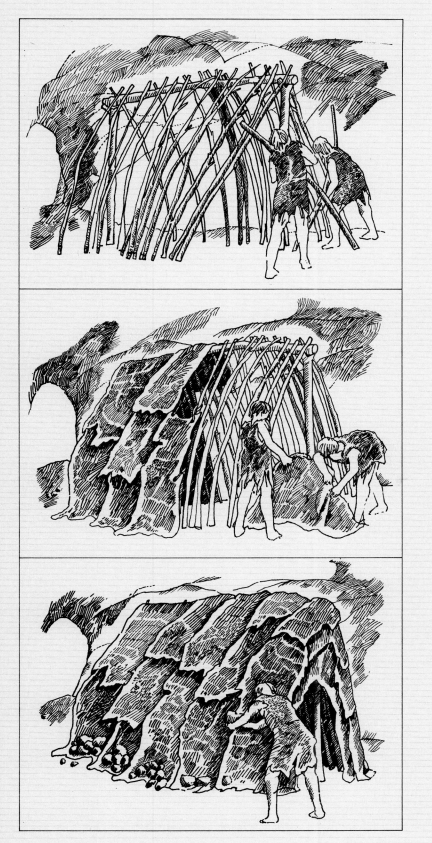

To make life more comfortable in clammy caves, Neanderthal man discovered how to build crude shelters like this one, using saplings and animal skins. Judging from the evidence of postholes on the floor of a cave in southern France, the shelter was constructed rather like a tent. In the top drawing, two Neanderthal workers lean side supports, stripped saplings, against a horizontal ridgepole that is supported at each end by upright poles set into holes dug in the ground. In the middle drawing, they cover the frame with layers of animal skins, lashing them to the saplings with thongs or simply hooking them onto the protruding stubs of branches. Finally (bottom), the men anchor the lower tier of skins with piles of stones to stabilize the structure and to seal off drafts.

outdoors. The game played by the two oldest boys is not frivolous. For hours at a time, they practice throwing spears and rocks at inanimate targets, perfecting their aim. Occasionally they charge toward a tree they have identified as an animal and beat it to death with their clubs. The women have little control over these two aspiring hunters and concentrate on their own chores. Wood must be gathered for the fire, and some precious meat must be dug up from the outdoor refrigerator. The hard life tells on them. The oldest looks 60, although she is only 45—and that is elderly by Neanderthal standards.

Far from home, the men search the forest-tundra. To cover the maximum territory, they separate into pairs and set off in different directions. No man hunts alone; a partner is needed to summon help in case one of the hunters suffers injury. One of these teams of hunters, having traveled northward for more than an hour, halts for the first time. The oldest man pulls a few hairs from his clothing and tosses them into the air to test the direction of the wind. It is essential to travel in a general upwind direction, because almost every creature in this land has an acute nose for the scent of man. When the men have taken their

Of several methods used by Neanderthal man to satisfy his taste for cooked meat, the one depicted here is familiar to any Boy Scout. It is based on a find at Pech de l'Aze in southern France, where archeologists came upon the remains of a large hearth paved with rocks that show signs of repeated heating—apparently a 50,000-year-old griddle made hot by building a roaring fire over the rocks (top drawing). After the rocks are heated, the fire is pushed to one side with a long, paddle-shaped stick (center). Chunks of meat are then placed on the hot stones (bottom) to cook, a process that would not only make the food more agreeable to eat but would also shorten the time spent in eating. And with quicker meals, Neanderthal man was free to engage in other worthwhile pursuits.

bearings, they set off again, keeping about 100 yards apart in order to sweep a broad area.

As they traverse the low hills in long, tireless strides, the hunters find tiny clues to the presence of game. There are the footprints and spoor of hares, the splayed tracks of a lynx, the spot where a fox has urinated, the torn bark on willow branches where elk have browsed and the smudged places in the snow where reindeer have fed.

Without warning, a clicking sound breaks the silence of the hunt. One of the men has struck two stones together. Instantly, the other hunter freezes. Silence. Then another click tells him to creep toward the spot where the signal was given. He joins his partner just below the crest of a hill and cautiously peers out to where his companion is pointing. Just ahead lies a lake. A herd of reindeer are resting on its frozen surface, chewing their cuds. This is a familiar sight here. The reindeer prefer the safety of open spaces where wolves and other predators can be detected at a distance. Later in the afternoon, the reindeer will wander along the wooded shore, sniffing for silvery lichens and scraping away the snow cover with their powerful forelegs to get at them. But the hunters need not wait until then. The reindeer

are swift creatures, in the woods or out in the open, capable of running at 30 miles per hour. Since the chase will be difficult no matter when or where it takes place, it might as well begin.

The men move stealthily down the hill and along the shore to get as close as they can without being observed. Then they burst into the open. In a flash, the reindeer are up and gone, galloping across the snow-covered ice and into the trees on the far shore. But one big-antlered buck is a little slower in getting to his feet than the others, hesitating just a fraction of a second before following the rest of the herd. Both hunters spot that hesitation and see the slight hitch in the buck's stride, indicating an infected hoof or an injured leg. They immediately realize that if they have a chance to catch any of the reindeer, the injured buck will be the one.

The chase lasts half an hour. Although the hunters run steadily, they lag far behind their prey most of the way. The swath of hoofprints leads in a wide circle. When the hunters are only a mile from home, they sight their target again. The buck is struggling through a snowdrift in a gully, snorting and kicking powder in all directions. The men close in and thrust their spears. With a last frenzied effort, the reindeer lunges out of the drift. One of the hunters has to dodge out of the way to avoid the slash of sharp antlers and hoofs, but two spears are protruding from the flanks of the animal, and the snow is stained by splotches of blood.

The second stage of the chase ends quickly. Following the erratic track of blood and hoofprints into a clump of trees, the hunters find the reindeer down on its knees, its head waving back and forth. The lead runner goes right up to the dying creature, lifts his club above its head and brings it down with such crushing force that the reindeer is dead almost as soon as the blow is struck.

Immediately, his partner heads for the cave to get butchering tools and bring the women back to help carry the meat. If the kill had taken place far from home, the hunters would have had to fashion butchering tools from whatever rocks could be found nearby; and they might have been forced to spend the night there, huddled in the snow, protecting the carcass from scavengers. But no such wait is necessary this time.

The sun is hanging just above the horizon when a triumphant parade of Neanderthal men and women reaches home again, carrying armloads of meat. The liver and fat are prized most of all, but the brain, kidney, heart and lungs will be eaten too. Bones will be split open to get at the marrow, and the soft head of the leg joints will be chewed. Even the vegetable contents of the reindeer's two stomachs will be consumed, with blood added to the foul-smelling mixture to make it more palatable.

Later, after the meal is over and darkness has descended, the entire band huddles around the fire. A baby sleeps in his mother's arms; a man begins to nod. Out on the forest-tundra, the struggle of creature against creature goes on without cease—claw, tooth, beak and muscle engaged in mortal combat all through the night.

A year in the life of a Neanderthal band contains many days like this one, although the fortunes of hunting vary greatly. During a two-week period later in the winter when a hard crust of snow covers the ground and seals off most forage, the hunters kill dozens of animals that have been weakened by starvation and disease. On other occasions, the men are away from the cave for days at a time, huddling under rock shelters at night, and still, despite their cunning, they return home empty-handed.

Spring approaches slowly, with cool cloudy weather at first and frequent lapses into the bitter grip of winter. Ice on the lake near the cave periodically emits great rolls of thunder as it shifts and cracks. But the snow shrinks visibly, and soon the growing season is in full swing again, decking out the forest in greenery. To escape the swarming insects, many of the grazing animals move toward the open tundra. This is a fine time for hunting, because the reindeer trot along predictable routes and are easily ambushed. More animals than can possibly be eaten are driven into bogs or pools and dispatched with clubs. Much of the meat is left to rot.

One day in May the Neanderthal band leaves the cave and heads north. All but a few stone tools are left behind, for it is easy to make new ones. Carrying babies, weapons, supplies of meat, and animal hides that will serve for tents, the men and women trudge along a river valley. At sunset each day they stop, rig up simple shelters and light fires with smouldering embers that have been brought along in a cup formed from a blob of soft clay—they do not know how to fashion pottery bowls.

As the Neanderthals journey onward, the trees begin to thin out, until there are only isolated stands of conifers and dwarf willow and birch. After a week of travel, the band reaches its summer domain. The previous autumn, when the Neanderthals left the open tundra, the vegetation was dun-colored, with patches of red and yellow. Now it is a vivid green again, lushly covered with grasses, low-lying shrubs and mats of mosses and lichens. Streams, ponds and lakes gleam in the sunshine. Tiny flowers bloom in colorful profusion.

During the sumptuous spring on the tundra, the band is better fed than at any other time of the year. The grazing animals are giving birth now, and the hunters take a number of calves. Huge flocks of geese, ducks and swans have flown in from the south, and many of them fall victim to well-aimed stones as they feed in the lakes and ponds. Each day, the women and children find downy baby birds in nests on the ground. Fish are taken by setting up weirs of branches in shallow pools. As the weeks pass the Neanderthals grow noticeably fatter.

Even at the height of summer, the weather remains rather cool, averaging about 50°F. The band lives in a hut made of animal hides stretched over a framework of branches and large animal bones. From time to time, the camp is moved to a new location, but each site is occupied long enough for split bones and unwanted food scraps to litter the area. The older boys keep a sharp eye on this refuse, hoping to surprise a muskrat or some other small creature that might be foolish enough to scavenge here.

Toward the end of summer, a tragedy occurs. A hunter, misjudging the strength left in a wounded bison, is badly gored while trying to deliver the *coup de grâce*. He is carried back to the camp, ashen-faced and bleeding. Poultices of herbs and clay do not avail against the deep chest-puncture, and within a few hours the hunter is dead. Early the next morning the dead man is buried, along with his club, spear and enough food for the journey into the world beyond the grave. When the burial is finished, the band leaves

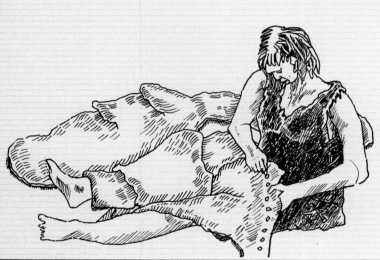

Neanderthals must have fashioned heavy clothing for the glacial cold of many of the regions in which they lived by using animal skins and stone tools as shown here. In the top drawing, a woman begins preparation of the clothing-to-be by cleaning the hide. Her tool is a stone scraper, and with it she removes stray bits of flesh and fat from inside the animal skin. After she has dried and cured the skin in the smoke of a smouldering fire, to toughen it and seal the pores, she cuts it into the desired shape with a stone knife. To assemble the garment (center) she first punches holes along the edge of the skin with a pointed stone, and then fits the garment to its wearer by lacing narrow strips of rawhide through the holes (bottom), creating a kind of ready-to-wear bearskin toga.

the camp. The dead man's wife moves to the bed of the bachelor hunter.

Summer on the tundra passes faster than anyone would wish. In September, the orgy of growth is over, and bright colors again begin to break out all across the land. The reindeer show signs of restlessness. In spring their antlers were soft and covered with the tender outer skin known as velvet, but now the blood supply to the velvet is cut off, and the animals seek out trees where they can rub their antlers to soothe the itching. The bulls engage in sparring matches and then mate with the cows.

One morning, after a light rain, the band wakes to discover that the tent is encrusted with ice. They too must head south. En route, they find more good hunting. Another band is met on the way and the two groups join forces. With every able-bodied man, woman and child taking part, the two bands succeed in stampeding an entire herd of horses over a cliff. This is the high point of the year, a time for relaxation and impromptu contests, and a time when marriageable young men and women might find a mate from the other band.

Days of intensive hunting lie ahead, but the animals will eventually grow wary. The storms of

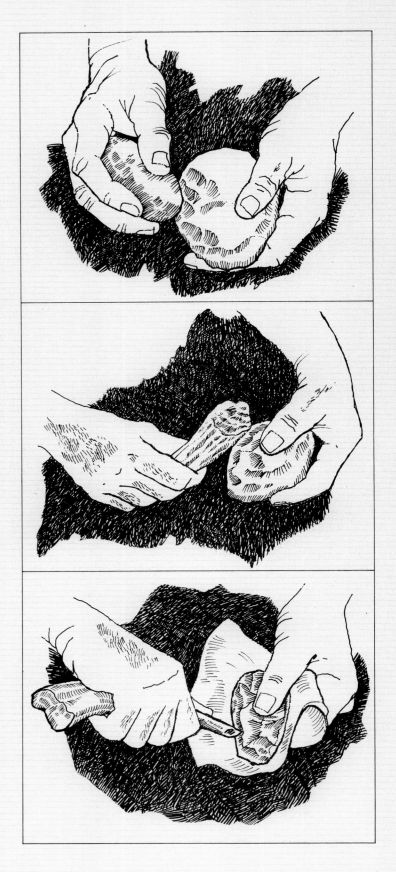

With a few strategically aimed blows, followed by some careful chipping, Neanderthal man fashioned himself a tool for cutting and scraping, exploiting the tendency of certain kinds of flint rock to fracture, like glass, in shell-shaped sections. In these pictures the toolmaker first rough-shapes the blade (top) by striking a piece of flint with a stone hammer, knocking off thick, scalloped flakes. He next uses a softer hammer of fire-hardened bone or antler to knock off flatter, more delicate flakes (center) to refine the edge and shape the tool to a contour suitable to the hand. Finally he finishes the edge to razor sharpness (bottom) by pressing the antler or bone against the ridges left by previous flakes. A cutter made this way is almost as effective as a steel knife.

winter will coop up the Neanderthals in their smoky cave. There will be sickness, perhaps death. But the band will still be there next spring and the spring after, holding onto this difficult northern land with the sort of fierce and indomitable grip reserved for those prizes that are hard won.

The picture of Neanderthal life afforded by this imagined journey backward in time may seem fanciful, but it is not fictional. Although the portrayal involves a certain amount of dramatic license, it is largely based on the sort of evidence that would be admissible in a court of law. It does not pretend to cover all people who lived in the world 60,000 years ago. It refers to a very special region—the open tundra and forest-tundra along the northernmost frontier of human settlement. What makes this region important is its adversity. The tundra country tested the mettle and resourcefulness of the Neanderthals to the utmost, and their success in coping with the difficulties imposed by the region marks an important milestone in man's efforts to conquer nature.

It should be remembered, of course, that most of the world's population in those days lived in less hostile environments, and their modes of survival were dissimilar in many respects to that of a band in the cold north. For example, the life of a band in the African savanna revolved around seasonal shifts of dry and rainy weather; the women collected a completely different array of grass seeds, fruits, insects, caterpillars, and perhaps honey or the edible gum of certain trees; the men killed antelope and zebras, instead of reindeer, woolly rhinoceroses and mammoths. Nevertheless, their hunting-and-gathering life style displayed many of the same basic features that characterized that of the Neanderthals in Germany.

How scientists come by the evidence that allows reconstruction of Neanderthal life is itself a fascinating story. One source is the study of life styles of contemporary hunter-gatherers—the few that still survive in the world today. Almost all of the current ideas about the social organization, hunting techniques and other facets of the life of early men are based on what we know of modern people who have not yet adopted agriculture. In trying to glimpse the past through the present, it is safest to stick to generalities, such as the observation that hunter-gatherers need a great deal of territory to get enough food or that the size of their bands averages about 25 individuals. But some more specific parallels between present-day hunter-gatherers and long-vanished Neanderthals can be cautiously drawn. For example, certain hunter-gatherers of Siberia, known as the Yukaghir, kill reindeer mainly by chasing them on foot for many miles across the snowy terrain and then summon their women to carry the carcasses home. It is at least plausible to assume that the Neanderthals of Germany did the same. The Yukaghir like to eat frozen berries, and it is reasonable to believe that Neanderthals shared this taste.

The model of contemporary hunting-and-gathering societies is not the only source of suppositions about the prehistory of mankind. Some of the key ingredients in the description of life in a Neanderthal band rest on solid documentary evidence. The presence of Mousterian tools in German geological deposits proves beyond doubt that Neanderthals did live there during the Würm glacial period. One especially well-excavated site near the town of Lebenstedt has supplied a wealth of information about the weather and vegetation at the edge of the northern tundra. No human fossils turned up at the site, but numerous fossilized animal bones were found, indicating that the Neanderthals hunted mostly reindeer but also went after mammoths, bison, horses and woolly rhinoceroses. A few remains of waterfowl, fish and mollusks were also discovered.

That the Neanderthals built artificial shelters when caves were unavailable to them is also known. While none have been found in Germany, a Neanderthal site 1,000 miles to the east, in Molodova, in the Soviet Union, has yielded clear evidence of a man-made shelter in open terrain. Of course, no one can say for sure that all northern Neanderthal bands constructed such huts; but it is much harder to conceive of their remaining ignorant of such an important adaptation to cold environments.

The open tundra was occupied only during the warmer months, rather than all year round, a point deduced from careful study of the Lebenstedt site. It indicates that Neanderthals lived there for a few weeks at a time during several summers. In winter, with few trees to fend off the freezing winds, conditions would have been unendurable; and in springtime the site was flooded by meltwaters. The

German band almost certainly retreated into the forest during the winter.

In some areas of Neanderthal life common sense is a guide. A good example is the assertion by some authorities that the women of the band used birch-bark containers when they gathered vegetable foods. All of the bark from that period has, of course, long since decayed. But almost all experts are agreed that mankind must have been using some sort of container from very earliest times, because women would hardly be so inefficient as to carry grain, nuts or berries back to their camp handful by handful. Birch bark was available in the forest-tundra, and it would have made fine containers for a band living there, but other materials may in fact have been used as well —animal skins or even the bladders or stomachs of animals would also have been satisfactory.

In time much more hard evidence about the Neanderthals' life—tools, fossils and other remains —should turn up to fill in missing details in the picture. In the meantime scientists have found ways to make the old evidence reveal new things. The slight amount of documentation that has survived from Neanderthal times is akin to a poem. With repeated readings and new modes of analysis, all sorts of hidden levels of meaning come to light. For example, Kenneth Weiss of the University of Michigan recently examined existing European Neanderthal skeletal material and found that the male fossils —easily identified by sexual differences in bone structure—outnumber the females by about 10 per cent. From this discovery, he concluded that the European Neanderthals practiced female infanticide. The most likely explanation would be that meat, procured by males, was more crucial to the band's survival than vegetable foods procured by females —necessitating an adjustment of the ratio of the sexes. In this case there is corroborating evidence: most European Neanderthal fossils show relatively little tooth wear, and it is known that a predominantly meat diet is much easier on the teeth than a diet that includes large amounts of tough-to-chew vegetable foods. Thus a dietary motive for infanticide may well have been present.

Even the most unlikely evidence occasionally turns out to be a sort of Rosetta stone. For instance, reindeer teeth have been used to show that some Neanderthals in southern France occupied their caves throughout the year. Reindeer are always born in the spring, and development of their teeth gives an accurate measure of their age. Caves have produced reindeer teeth of all different ages, proving that the animals were killed during spring, summer, autumn and winter. This is no trivial finding. The evidence that these Neanderthals could get enough food without having to move about in a large territory testifies to a high level of hunting prowess. Probably only the inhabitants of the very richest lands could afford to lead a nonnomadic existence. In most places, camps had to be shifted from time to time as the game supply became depleted or when the weather became intolerable—or even because of the accumulation of garbage.

Some of the most intriguing information about the Neanderthals is the least obvious. In the 1950s, F. E. Koby studied some Neanderthal front teeth under a microscope and spotted hundreds of parallel scratches in the enamel. These scratches seem certainly to be a result of eating habits. The Neanderthals, like modern-day Eskimos and other hunter-gatherers,

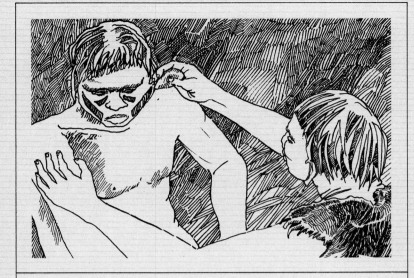

To increase his luck in hunting, Neanderthal apparently wore magic markings of natural pigments—red ocher and black manganese oxide, both of which exist in many parts of the world. Hand-shaped lumps of raw pigment and traces of color found inside hollow bones and rocks suggest that symbols were applied in the three ways shown here. In the top drawing, a man uses a lump of pigment to draw directly on his subject's skin. In the middle drawing the pigment, powdered in a Stone Age mortar and mixed with water or grease, is daubed on with a wad of fibers. At bottom, the designer blows powdered pigment through a length of reed or hollowed-out bone—probably relying on the oily accretions of his subject's skin to fix the magic marking in place.

stuffed meat into their mouths, clamped it between their teeth and cut off the excess with stone knives. The knives produced diagonal scratches—which were seen to run from upper left to lower right. Since it can be assumed that the Neanderthals would use their more adept hand to wield the stone knife and the other hand to hold the end of the meat, the direction of the scratches is one of the indications that these Neanderthals were right-handed.

A natural reaction to this discovery might be: "So what?" Actually, the indication of hand preference of the Neanderthals may represent an important clue to human history. In the entire animal kingdom, only man favors one hand over the other. Some scientists are beginning to suspect that the development of handedness is intimately related to the development of speech. The suspicion is based on complicated neurological studies, but if these scientists are indeed right in their assumption, those little scratches on some old front teeth may well be an oblique reference to something of great portent—the Neanderthals' command of language.

One of the most provocative—and controversial —studies of Neanderthals made in recent years tackled this very subject from a completely different angle—and with completely different results. In 1971 Philip Lieberman of the University of Connecticut and Edmund Crelin of Yale attempted to bring those long-ago voices within hearing distance again. They began an investigation of the linguistic capabilities of the Neanderthals by making a series of measurements of the neck vertebrae and base of the skull of the fossil found at La Chapelle-aux-Saints in France. These measurements were used to determine the formation of the vocal tract—the air passages in the nose, mouth and throat that produce speech by opening and closing in complex ways in order to vary the simple tones generated by the voice box, or larynx. The measurements suggested that Neanderthal man lacked a modern kind of pharynx—the chamber behind the mouth and above the larynx. As a result, the man from La Chapelle-aux-Saints was unable to utter the vowel sounds heard in the words bar, boo, beep and bought; nor could he form the consonants g and k. His repertoire of sounds was quite impoverished compared to that of modern humans, consisting of fewer consonants and a relatively narrow range of vowel sounds—those heard by us in such English words as bit, bet, bat and but.

These findings have been vigorously disputed, and no one is yet certain exactly what they mean. Perhaps Neanderthal man could communicate quite well with his own kind of speech; on the other hand, he may have been capable of only very limited verbal communication. Curiously enough, Neanderthals outside of western Europe may have possessed a more efficient speaking apparatus. Lieberman and Crelin have extended their study and determined that Rhodesian man in Africa had a slightly more modern pharynx than that of the man from La Chapelle-aux-Saints. And a fossil from the site of Skhul in the Middle East had a nearly modern vocal tract.

If Lieberman and Crelin are right and the voices of a long-vanished people can indeed be summoned from old bones, who knows what else is possible? Someday we may know the Neanderthals as well as we now know the Mayas or the Sumerians.

The Far-flung Worlds
of a Rugged Breed

Canyons like this one, cut by glacial torrents, existed in Europe in Neanderthal's time.

Neanderthal man, far more than his predecessors, achieved the mastery over nature that was becoming the hallmark of the human race. The vicissitudes of climate and terrain, which dictated where animals and plants could prosper, still influenced how he lived—but they did not necessarily determine where he lived. Only the desolation of the ice sheets themselves defeated him. Everywhere else he went in a world that was repeatedly altered by glaciations, he managed to adapt, learning to get along in environments that ranged from tundra to desert fringes.

Between 45,000 and 75,000 years ago—one of the coldest periods of the Würm glaciation—Neanderthal man was forced to cope with an unusual variety of locales and climates (map, page 38). He developed a corresponding diversity of living styles, altering his diet, hunting practices, clothing and shelter accordingly. He succeeded in using some unlikely places—even the deep canyon pictured at left, though uninviting as a permanent home, could have served for overnight shelter in his wanderings. For in spite of its cool dampness, this cleft in the rocks had one big advantage: it offered safety from predators.

The Frozen Tundra

As glaciation increased during the Würm, the stark, frigid tundra spread southward from the north to cover enormous portions of what is now France and Germany and to extend into parts of Asia and the Middle East. For most of the year, storms blanketed the ground with snow and ice, which melted in spring and flooded the low-lying ground. In summer temperatures rarely rose above 50° F.

Bleak and hostile as tundra seems, it offered Neanderthal a ready supply of meat—in vast herds of hardy reindeer. Also present here were woolly mammoths, rhinos and Siberian ibex. During spring and summer, flocks of migrating geese, ducks and swans arrived to nest and breed—and further enrich Neanderthal's diet.

Because of the tundra weather, Neanderthal sought shelter in caves, using animal skins to curtain the entrances of small rock shelters, or building temporary structures inside the larger ones. In open areas, he erected tents of animal skins and huddled around fires. Furs were used for body garments and footgear.

Multicolored leaves of dwarf birches brighten the gray landscape of tundra in early September when

temperatures hover above freezing. The plants consist primarily of bushes, grasses, mosses and lichens best adapted to the short growing season.

The Mountain Meadowlands

Neanderthal man probably encountered conditions similar to those in today's temperate zones when he ventured into southwestern Europe. Here, in what now are semiarid lands, he found open grasslands and many lakes and ponds—a moist, fertile environment nurtured in part by snow on mountains nearby. The winters were cold and snowy, but the summers were sunny and the temperatures mild. Although the rhinoceroses of the tundra were not common in these uplands, the meadows supported wild cattle and deer, the lakes otters and many waterfowl.

The relatively comfortable climate permitted the Neanderthals to live in foothill caves or rock shelters, or even to set up conical tents of animal skins in the open. But in winter, the fur-hide clothing worn by men farther north was still essential.

Scattered groves of trees dot meadowland where tall grass grows waist-high. Small lakes, formed by

springs, and also fed by melting snow from the nearby mountains, created livable environments in Neanderthal times in areas that are now semiarid.

The cliff-lined edges of the Mediterranean Sea, along parts of North Africa, the Middle East and southern Europe, attracted Neanderthal man, who

The Coastal Cliffs

Neanderthal man apparently lived all around the Mediterranean Sea, which receded during the cold spells to expose many more cliff headlands than exist in the region today. Riddled with deep caves, these coastal areas provided ready-made homes.

The climate, though cooler than it is now, was relatively dry and comfortable year-round. Patches of conifers, heather and juniper grew along the coasts and lured elephants, horses and goats. Neanderthal may also have varied his diet of game with fish or shellfish from the sea's salty waters.

ound comfortable dwelling places in the caves that the sea had carved into the porous limestone.

Scrubby grass, low bushes, thorn trees and spiny, pulpy succulents flourish on the borderline between arid desert and the wetter, richer country

nearby. Such fringe areas expanded greatly during Neanderthal times as worldwide rainfall lessened.

The Fringe of the Desert

The climate changes that brought glaciers to the north locked up so much of the earth's water supply in mile-thick ice sheets that the moisture available for precipitation was sharply reduced; far to the south the rainfall decreased markedly, and what had been savanna country dried up into near-desert.

The semiarid fringe areas around many deserts expanded, particularly in East Africa. But temperatures remained tropical and from the foothills of the mountains in the desert flowed the streams and springs that attracted such targets of the southern Neanderthal hunters as gazelles, antelopes and Cape buffalo.

Light reaching the floor of openings like this in a tropical rain forest encouraged the growth of rich vegetation, and it was this food resource rather

A Clearing in the Rain Forest

The lush rain forests of equatorial Africa and Asia, although diminished by the arid conditions resulting from the worldwide cooling-off, remained dense and difficult of access during Neanderthal times. The climate in such regions was much as it is today, with temperatures in the eighties—and a little rain every day.

Despite these uncomfortable conditions, there is evidence that Neanderthals, using stone tools especially devised for cutting wood, chopped their way into the forest. Game would have been scarce and almost impossible to hunt in the tangled undergrowth, so the Neanderthals venturing here presumably were foraging for vegetables—and perhaps snacks of the forest's rich insect life.

han the few forest animals that apparently motivated some Neanderthals to penetrate the jungle.

The Open Forest of the Savanna

Neanderthal man found his most comfortable home during the Würm ice age in the partially wooded, parklike environment of the savanna—the kind of country that had given rise to the earliest humans. In Africa these congenial regions grew in size as drier conditions transformed dense forest into tree-dotted grassland. A narrow fringe of savanna bordered the arid Sahara to the north, while broad expanses covered much of the eastern, sub-Saharan portion of the continent, but there were also huge areas of savanna all around the Mediterranean and in eastern Asia.

The weather on the grasslands was warm and sunny, and except for short rainy spells in winter, there was little climate change from season to season —and no need for clothing or shelter. In Africa Neanderthal camped out at night in the open around fires kept burning to frighten away predator cats, and by day hunted zebras, giraffes, hippos, baboons and apes.

The tropical savanna, whose gentle contours are carpeted with tall grasses and dotted with trees.

ome nut-bearing, was the Garden of Eden of the ice age, providing Neanderthal man with a delightful climate and plentiful supplies of food.

Chapter Four: A Stirring of Human Spirit

Every once in a while, like a secret panel sliding open at the touch of a hidden button, the past unveils some astonishing example of human precocity—a Viking dwelling in Newfoundland, glorious Indian temples in the tangled jungles of Central America, man-made tools in geological deposits two million years old. The study of the Neanderthals has produced more than its share of such stunning moments. Generations of anthropologists, knowing the Neanderthals were primitive, and prepared to believe they were something less than human, repeatedly were confounded by evidence to the contrary. By now, discovery after discovery has shown that these ancient people are due the honor accorded human pioneers, for they inaugurated some of the activities and beliefs that are considered most characteristic of mankind. The Neanderthals conceived of a life after death. They cared for aged and handicapped individuals. They attempted to control their own destiny through magical rites. And they may even have taken the first hesitant steps into the realm of art and symbolmaking. In fact, it seems they were the first human beings to display the complete spectrum of behavior that can be considered to constitute human nature.

Of all the various indications of the precocious behavior of the Neanderthals, their practice of burying the dead is the best documented and easiest to interpret. Death is life's bitterest fact, the inescapable

Propped up against a stone pillow, the body of an aged Neanderthal man is launched into the afterlife with a funeral feast. The scene reconstructs a funeral that took place some 40,000 or more years ago at La Chapelle-aux-Saints, France: the grave of an old man, with a stone pillow and the bone from a chunk of meat, was found there in 1908. The formality of this and other ancient cave burials is evidence that Neanderthals thought about the meaning of life and death.

defeat at the end of a long struggle to survive and prosper, and man is not the only creature saddened by it. Many animals seem momentarily distraught when death claims one of their number; elephants, for instance, have been observed trying to revive a dying member of the herd, even attempting to get it back on its feet by lifting it with their tusks. But only man anticipates the event far in advance, acknowledging that it will inevitably occur, dreading it, refusing to accept it as conclusive and taking some solace in a belief in an afterlife. One mark of this belief is burial of the dead.

The Neanderthals were not credited with deliberately meaningful burial of their dead until more than a half-century after their discovery. The original Neanderthal man taken from the cave in the Neander Valley of Germany was almost certainly buried by his survivors, although no one suspected so when the bones were found in 1856. The two fossils discovered at Spy in Belgium in 1885 were also buried; apparently fires were lighted over the bodies, perhaps in an effort to counteract the chill of death. But once again no one guessed that Spy had been the scene of an ancient burial. Then in 1908 the cave of La Chapelle-aux-Saints in France almost shouted its evidence of a Neanderthal funeral rite. The excavators found an ancient hunter who had been carefully laid out in a shallow trench. A bison leg was placed on his chest, and the trench was filled with broken animal bones and flint tools. These various articles might readily have been seen as provisions for the world beyond the grave, since many primitive peoples bury their dead with food, weapons and other goods. And yet even then most experts failed to make the connection that now seems obvious.

But the evidence continued to turn up. In 1912, two more Neanderthal graves were found at the nearby site of La Ferrassie. The men who carried out the excavation wrote: "We have been able to recognize, at the base of the Mousterian layer, the existence of two small trenches measuring 70 centimeters wide by 30 centimeters in depth, very precisely cut in half-sphere form in the underlying red-yellowish loamy gravel, filled with a mixture of nearly equal parts of the black earth of the Mousterian fireplace above and of the underlying gravel. The existence of artificially dug graves was absolutely obvious. . . . This is, then, in the clearest way, proof of a funeral rite. The point has been disputed. These excavations establish it in a manner that cannot permit any doubt."

The excavation of the La Ferrassie site took many years, and the complete results were not published until 1934. This rock shelter appears to have served as a family cemetery. Six Neanderthal fossils were eventually exhumed—a man, a woman, two children about five years old and two infants. Also found were several trenches that seemed to have been graves but lay empty, perhaps because the bones had somehow decomposed or the bodies had been dug up by a scavenging animal such as a cave hyena. Flint flakes and bone splinters had been put in the grave of the adult male, and a flat stone slab had been placed over his shoulders and head (to protect him? to restrain him from coming back to life?). The woman was buried in a sort of exaggerated fetal position, with her legs tightly bent at the knees and pulled up against her chest. It looked as if thongs had been used to bind her legs before her corpse stiffened. This flexing, as the folding of legs is called, occurs in many Neanderthal burials. Religious beliefs may account for the practice. Many primitive peoples tie up the dead in order to prevent them from coming back to bother the living. However, some experts believe that flexing was merely a way of saving labor in the arduous work of hacking a trench in rocky ground with stone or wooden tools. A grave could be considerably smaller if the dead person were flexed instead of stretched out full length.

The most perplexing grave at La Ferrassie was located in the rear of the shelter. Here the lower skeleton and skull of a child were interred in a gently sloping trench—but they were separated by a distance of about three feet. The skull was covered by a triangular limestone slab whose underside displayed a number of cup-shaped impressions, possibly symbolic markings of some sort. Why were the head and the rest of the body separated? One authority, the Abbé Bouyssonnie, a French prehistorian, has suggested that the child was killed and beheaded by a wild animal; later, the head was intentionally buried upslope from the body so that, in the afterlife, it might somehow find its way down the declivity and rejoin the trunk. This is the purest surmise, but there must be some reason for the odd arrangement.

As more and more Neanderthal graves were found over the years, a larger puzzle emerged. It relates not to the meaning of specific funeral rites but to the identity of the people who performed them. Almost every

While a mother mourns, a Neanderthal father places the last of three flint offerings in the grave of their child, buried at La Ferrassie, France. The curious circular grave, later domed over, is one of a cluster of nine arranged mysteriously in orderly rows of three. Although eight of the graves were empty when discovered in 1909, the skeletons of five other bodies were nearby in trenches in the same shallow cave, which apparently had been set aside to solemnize burials.

Neanderthal burial in western Europe is associated with a certain toolmaking tradition known as Quina-Ferrassie. Yet this tradition is only one of four main styles that the leading expert on Neanderthal tools, François Bordes, believes were used in western Europe. In addition to the Quina-Ferrassie style (containing a high proportion of flake tools used for scraping), there are Denticulate Mousterian (containing many notched or toothed flakes), Typical Mousterian (highly developed pointed tools) and Mousterian of Acheulean tradition (a very diverse tool kit that includes numerous hand axes). In Bordes' opinion, these four basic sorts of tool kits represent distinct cultures—different peoples occupying the same general area but having little contact with one another. But no bones have been found associated with Denticulate tools. And no fossils have been found in association with tools of the Mousterian of Acheulean tradition (M.A.T., in archeological shorthand). Did only the Quina-Ferrassie people believe in a life after death? Not necessarily. Burial is not the only ritual way of entering the afterworld. Bordes speculates that the people of the other tool styles may have exposed corpses to the elements on platforms outside their caves or placed them in trees, as some modern tribesmen still do. Or they could have practiced cremation, which is an excellent solution to the problem of frozen ground. These and many other techniques for dealing with the dead are perfectly compatible with a spiritual belief in an afterlife.

No matter what the answer to this European puzzle, many other Neanderthals in the world buried their dead. Far to the east, on the Crimean peninsula that juts into the Black Sea, the graves of two individuals were found at a cave at Kiik-Koba in 1924.

One trench held the remains of a year-old child resting on his side with his legs bent. This skeleton was in poor condition because later inhabitants of this cave had dug a trench for their fire directly over the grave and inadvertently disturbed the bones. Three feet away from the child was the grave of a man, also lying on his side with his legs tucked up. The body was oriented east-west—as were the Spy fossils and five out of six of the Ferrassie fossils. Possibly the orientation signified something about the rising or setting sun.

The early 1930s saw the discovery of a magnificent set of Neanderthal fossils at Mount Carmel above Haifa in Israel (page 23). On the terrace beyond the mouth of the cave of Mugharet es-Skhul in the mountain, five men, two women and three children had been placed in shallow graves. All of the bodies had their legs pulled up so tightly that their feet touched their buttocks. However, there is little other suggestion of ceremony—with a single startling exception. One 45-year-old man held in his arms the jawbones of a huge boar. Did the boar cause his death? Or do the jaws represent a hunting trophy, proclaiming the man's prowess to whatever spirits might meet him in the afterlife?

The ambiguous chord struck by this burial is echoed at another site farther to the east, in the mountains of Uzbek in central Asia. Here, in 1938, the cave of Teshik-Tash surrendered the body of a Neanderthal boy. Although his grave had been damaged by an animal, a few enigmatic signs of a funeral rite survived. Six pairs of goat horns, still attached to their skulls, were pushed into the cave floor in a roughly circular arrangement around the grave. Some interpreters maintain the horns were merely digging tools, but their placement in a rough circle makes a ritualistic significance seem plausible. Whatever the circle of horns means, it is a tribute to the hunting skills of the Neanderthals. Catching the elusive, agile goats in this precipitous region must have been quite a feat even for these experienced hunters.

The most amazing Neanderthal burial of all came to light in 1960 at the Shanidar cave in the rugged Zagros Mountains of northern Iraq. There Ralph Solecki of Columbia University dug down through compressed deposits to uncover a total of nine Neanderthals, some of them apparently killed by rocks falling from the ceiling. At the very back of the cave, in a layer estimated to be 60,000 years old, he found the grave of a hunter with a badly crushed skull.

As a routine procedure, Solecki collected samples of the soil in and around the grave and sent them to a laboratory at the Musée de l'Homme in France. There his colleague Arlette Leroi-Gourhan checked the pollen content, hoping it would provide useful information on the climate and vegetation prevailing during Neanderthal times. What she found was utterly unexpected. Pollen was present in the grave in unprecedented abundance. Even more astonishing, some of it appeared in clusters and a few clusters had been preserved along with the parts of the flowers that had supported them. No birds or animals or wind could possibly have deposited such material there. Clearly, masses of flowers had been placed in the grave by the companions of the dead man. Leroi-Gourhan believes that the Neanderthal hunter was laid to rest on a woven bedding of pine boughs and flowers; more blossoms may very well have been strewn over his body.

Microscopic examination of the pollen indicated that it came from numerous species of bright-colored flowers, related to the grape hyacinth, bachelor's button, hollyhock and groundsel. Some of these plants are used in poultices and herbal remedies by contemporary peoples in Iraq. Perhaps the Neanderthals, too, felt that the blossoms possessed medicinal properties and added them to the grave in an effort to restore health to the fallen hunter in the afterlife. On the other hand, the flowers may have been put there in the same spirit that moves modern people to place them on graves and gravestones.

The Neanderthals must have sensed the precious quality of life more keenly than any creatures before them, because funeral rites, at the most fundamental level, represent a commitment to human conservation. Funerals declare that some essential quality of human life—call it spirit or soul—cannot be destroyed, but continues to exist after death, somewhere else, in some other form.

This growing sense of the value of life is reflected not only in death rites but also in the Neanderthals' treatment of old or handicapped individuals. The man of La Chapelle-aux-Saints, for instance, was long past his prime when he died. His skeleton reveals that he had been bent over by arthritis and could not possibly have taken part in a hunt. Even the act of eating must have been difficult for him, since he had lost all but two teeth. Had he lived at some earlier time, he probably would have been abandoned to starve after his economic usefulness to the group was spent. But the Neanderthals evidently were not ruled by such stern logic. This man's companions unselfishly provided food, and they probably even softened it for him by partially chewing it.

Bunches of Stone Age bachelor's buttons, grape hyacinths and hollyhocks are strewn over a dead Neanderthal by grieving members of his hunting band, while others gather to recall his exploits and brave deeds. The remains of the man were unearthed at Shanidar, Iraq, in 1960, but not until earth samples were analyzed did anyone realize that flowers played a part in Neanderthal burials. The samples proved to contain pollen from flowers and a thick pallet of pine boughs.

The Neanderthals' concern for the handicapped is suggested also by remains at Shanidar. Some of the Neanderthal bones found there belonged to a 40-year-old man who probably was killed by a rockfall. Study of his skeleton revealed that before his accidental death he had had the use of only one arm. His right arm and shoulder were poorly developed—probably a birth defect. Despite the major disability, he lived to a ripe age for a Neanderthal. His front teeth are unusually worn, suggesting that he spent much of his time chewing animal hides to soften them for use as clothes, or used his teeth in lieu of his arm in order to hold objects.

The fact that the Neanderthals could find a place in their society for aged or handicapped individuals does not necessarily mean that they were paragons of kindness, brimming with love for their fellow man. At Neanderthal sites there is plentiful evidence for the darker side of human nature. For example, a fossil found at Skhul bore the traces of a fatal spear wound. The point of a wooden spear, long since decayed, had passed through the top of the man's thigh bone and the socket of the hip bone, ending up inside the pelvic cavity.

Another ancient act of violence is recorded in the Shanidar deposits. One of the ribs of a Neanderthal fossil from the Iraq cave was deeply grooved by the point of a weapon, probably a wooden spear. The tip had penetrated the man's chest and perhaps punctured a lung—but this hunter somehow survived the wound, for the bone shows signs of healing. The original Neanderthal from Germany also had survived a grievous injury, although his recovery was incomplete: his left elbow bones were so misshapen that he could not have raised his hand to his mouth—but

whether the damage was done by man or beast will never be known.

T. Dale Stewart of the Smithsonian Institution has noted an interesting correspondence between the injuries of the men from Skhul, Shanidar and the Neander Valley. All three wounds involved the left side of the body. This is the side that would tend to be most easily injured if there were combat between right-handed opponents.

That Neanderthals sometimes killed one another should surprise no one. Perhaps more surprising is the ample evidence that they also ate one another. In 1899 the mutilated remains of about 20 Neanderthals —men, women and children—were found at the site of Krapina in Yugoslavia. Skulls had been smashed into fragments; limb bones had been split lengthwise (presumably for their marrow); and there were traces of charring to hint that the human meat had been cooked. In 1965 another collection of charred and shattered human bones—again involving at least 20 individuals—was found at the cave of Hortus in France. The remains were mixed up with other animal bones and food refuse, as if some ancient inhabitants of the cave had drawn no distinction between human meat and that of a bison or reindeer.

Some anthropologists feel that the cannibalism at Krapina and Hortus was motivated by nothing more than hunger. They suggest that a band of Neanderthals, having run short of other game, simply decided that the neighbors would make a nice meal.

The people-for-lunch idea does not get much support from a study by Stanley M. Garn and Walter D. Block, physical anthropologists at the University of Michigan, who looked at the problem of cannibalism from the viewpoint of practical dietetics, attempting to determine whether or not human flesh is a good source of nutrition. According to the arithmetic of the two anthropologists, the edible muscle mass of a 110-pound man would yield about 10 pounds of useful protein, provided that he was skillfully butchered —not very much food, compared to the meat of a mammoth or a bison.

In historic times, hunger has rarely been the reason for cannibalism. Contemporary peoples who practice cannibalism are not driven by anything so crude as hunger or blind ferocity. They eat their fellow humans for ritualistic reasons. In some societies, men believe that they can acquire strength and courage by eating the flesh of an enemy. There are also documented cases of murderers eating the flesh of their victim in order to prevent the ghost of the dead man from haunting them; the relatives of the murdered man may also eat his flesh, believing that it will aid them in their quest for revenge. However, the slaughters at Krapina and Hortus seem to have been more savage and less selective than any cannibalistic rite of today.

Ritualistic motives appear more likely at another ancient feast on human flesh. The evidence for this one turned up on the banks of the Solo River in Java, in gravel and sand deposits thought to be more than 100,000 years old—and possibly quite a bit older. Eleven skulls were dug up, but no other skeletal parts were found except for two leg bones. The facial bones had been smashed off every skull, and not a single jaw or tooth was left.

The body-less isolation of the skulls is enough to hint at some ritual intent. Even more suggestive is the treatment of the opening at the base of the skull, known as the foramen magnum. This opening, where the spinal cord connects to the brain, is normally about an inch and a half in diameter. In all but two of the Solo skulls, the foramen magnum had been widened considerably by hacking at the bony edges with stone or wooden tools. Similar mutilation of skulls has been observed among modern cannibals, who widen the opening so they can reach into the skulls, scoop out the brains and eat them.

Not all authorities accept a direct connection between cannibalism and the widening of the foramen magnum. Certain contemporary peoples keep skulls as trophies or as cherished mementos of departed relatives. They clean the skulls by opening up the base and removing the brain. However, it is doubtful that any of the skulls from Java were cherished, because, in every case, the face was knocked off, and at least one of the men was killed by a crushing blow to the back of the head.

Body-less skulls of Neanderthals have been found in Europe as well as Asia, prompting speculation about a worldwide Neanderthal skull cult. One skull, belonging to a five- or six-year-old child, turned up in a cave on the Rock of Gibraltar. The discoverer, struck by the absence of any other human bones, suggested that it had been placed there as a trophy or sacred relic. A similar find occurred at Ehringsdorf, Germany. Here, the jaw of an adult, the remains of a 10-year-old child and the cranium of a woman were unearthed. The woman had been repeatedly clubbed on the forehead; her head was severed from the body; and, as at Solo, the foramen magnum had been enlarged. Although some experts believe these skulls could have been brought to their strange state by natural causes—hyenas, the pressure of rock, and so on

—another skull, from Monte Circeo in Italy, would seem to resolve such doubts.

Monte Circeo is a limestone hill located on a peninsula about 55 miles south of Rome. According to Greek mythology, this spot is the place where Circe, the beautiful but sinister daughter of Apollo, turned passing sailors into beasts, sparing only Odysseus. During Roman times, Monte Circeo was a popular coastal resort, and the ruins of ancient villas can still be seen amid the flowering shrubs on the slopes. Twentieth Century tourist trade was responsible for the discovery of a Neanderthal sanctuary, hidden far beneath these slopes.

In 1939 the owner of a seaside inn decided to expand his premises to accommodate his steadily increasing trade. When workmen dug into the limestone to make room for a bigger terrace, they bared the entrance of a cave, about 15 feet above sea level. Apparently the cave had been sealed off by a landslide long ago, transforming it into a pristine time vault such as archeologists dream of. The proprietor of the inn and several of his friends crept on their hands and knees along a narrow corridor leading into the hillside. The corridor opened onto a chamber where no man had set foot for perhaps 60,000 years. The chamber turned out to be a weird sanctuary. By lantern light the explorers could see that a shallow trench had been scooped out of the ground near the farthest wall. A single skull rested there, surrounded by an oval ring of stones.

Subsequent examination of the skull showed that it was Neanderthal and that the man had been killed by a blow to the temple. And once again, the foramen magnum had been enlarged. This mutilation, plus the presence of the ring of stones, provided plain evidence that a ceremony had been staged in the cave.

The stone-encircled skull at Monte Circeo could signify almost anything. Consider the following rite of some contemporary head-hunting tribes in New Guinea: when a child is born, these people kill a man from another tribe; the father or a near relative of the infant beheads the victim, opens the foramen magnum to extract the brain, which is then baked with sago, a starch made from the pith of a palm, and eaten. All this is done in the belief that the newborn child cannot be assigned a name without the ritual treatment of the brain of a man whose name is known (an anonymous corpse would not do at all). This violent rite is so alien to Western culture that its explanation seems incredible, despite the testimony of eyewitnesses. The practice could not possibly be guessed at if there were only a mutilated skull and some sago to go by. Thus, although it does no harm to speculate about the rite at Monte Circeo, the chances of being correct are not much better than those of a New Guinean hunter trying to guess why men in the Western world traditionally launch a ship by breaking a bottle of champagne across the bow.

Neanderthal man's rites of burial and cannibalism may be only the visible tip of an iceberg of hidden ceremonies. Practically all known primitive peoples have special beliefs and practices pertaining to key

Enshrined in a small cave of its own, ringed with a circle of stones, a skull directs empty eyes toward the activities of the Neanderthal family who put it there. The skull may have been a symbol of an honored spirit guarding those left behind; it was discovered face down in a cave at Mount Circeo, Italy, its position suggesting that long ago it had toppled from a supporting stick. The natural aperture at the base had been enlarged, perhaps to remove the brain for ritual cannibalism.

steps in the human life cycle, and it is at least reasonable to assume that the Neanderthals did too. Birth, for instance, may have been treated as more than a purely biological event. Perhaps the Neanderthals had ritualistic ways of ensuring the safety of the mother, welcoming the child into the world, giving it a name and aiding its chances of good fortune later in life. Other likely occasions for ceremonies were the attainment of puberty, the initiation of hunters, marriage or the choice of a leader. Serious illness, too, might have called for a special attempt to enlist help from the gods or to drive malevolent spirits from the body of the afflicted person. And death, of course, stirred the ritual impulse most deeply of all.

Anthropologists feel quite certain that the Neanderthals, like modern hunter-gatherers, had rites related to hunting. The outcome of the hunt affected every individual—both sexes and all ages. It was a matter of great urgency that the supply of animals remain plentiful and that the men of the band enjoy good luck and personal safety in the hunt. But nothing in their world was guaranteed. Hunters could be injured. A long spell of bad weather could cut down on the catch. Animal herds might be decimated by disease, changes in the predator population or a host of other ecological factors. Mysterious forces operating beyond the horizon could interfere with animal migrations, causing herds to disappear.

Prior to the Neanderthal era, these various liabilities were probably regarded as being largely beyond human control. But the Neanderthals apparently attempted to manipulate hidden forces of their universe that controlled success and failure in the hunt. They seem to have practiced hunting magic. One clue to their efforts comes from the so-called Cave of Witch-es, west of Genoa, Italy. In the depths of the cave, almost 1,500 feet from the entrance, Neanderthal hunters threw pellets of clay at a stalagmite that has a vague animal shape. The inconvenient location of the stalagmite rules out the possibility that this was merely a game or a kind of target practice. The fact that the men went so far back into the cave to throw the pellets suggests that the activity had magical meaning of some kind.

In 1970, Ralph Solecki discovered evidence of a deer ceremony at a cave in Lebanon. Here, about 50,000 years ago, some Neanderthals dismembered a fallow deer, placed the meat on a bed of stones and sprinkled it with red ocher. The natural pigment was almost certainly intended as a symbol of blood—the blood of the earth, in a sense. The rite seems to represent a ritualistic or magical attempt to control life and death in the deer kingdom.

The most famous example of Neanderthal hunting magic is the bear cult. It came to light when a German archeologist, Emil Bächler, excavated the cave of Drachenloch between 1917 and 1923. Located 8,000 feet up in the Swiss Alps, the cave tunnels deep into a mountainside. The front part served as an occasional dwelling place for Neanderthals. Farther back, Bächler found a cubical chest made of stones and measuring approximately three and a quarter feet on a side. The top of the chest was covered by a single massive slab of stone. Inside were seven bear skulls, all arranged with their muzzles facing the cave entrance. Still deeper in the cave, six bear skulls were found set in niches along the walls. Some had the bones of limbs next to them but the skull and the adjacent bones did not always come from the same bear. In one of these skulls, a leg bone had been thrust through the arch of the cheekbone—an arrangement that must have been made by human agency. The Drachenloch find is not unique. At the site of Regourdu in southern France, a rectangular pit, covered by a flat stone slab weighing nearly a ton, held the bones of more than 20 bears. The object of these rites was a now-extinct species, *Ursus spelacous,* known as a cave bear. This barrel-chested brute outweighed a grizzly and measured nine feet from nose to tail. Swift, powerful and less predictable than any herd animal, it occupied a difficult environment, wintering in caves and ranging throughout the rugged, densely wooded sections of the European mountains during the milder seasons of the year.

From what is known of bear behavior and bear-hunting techniques of some modern peoples, it is possible to imagine the course of a Neanderthal battle with the cave bear. Picture a group of half a dozen hunters heading up into the mountains in February. The timing of the battle is in their favor. Roused from its winter sleep, the bear will be groggy and somewhat weakened by depletion of its reserves of fat, but even at this season it possesses strength enough to smash skulls, snap wooden lances and toss human bodies about almost effortlessly.

These hunters know the location of every cave in their land, and during the previous weeks they have scouted each one to determine what sort of animal is wintering inside. The reconnoitering phase was fairly safe. A rock or torch could be thrown into the caves to elicit growls for identification—lion, hyena, female bear with cubs or, finally, a solitary male bear. The man who located the animal did not disturb it further on that occasion, but returned to camp. Now he and his fellow hunters march straight to their destination, threading their way up through the trees, past rivers of ice and along ridges where plumes of wind-driven snow fly off into space and down into dizzying valleys below.

They reach the cave at midday, when the snow glare will work to their advantage, blinding the animal as it rushes out into the light. Two of the men gather heavy rocks and station themselves on a ledge over the cave entrance. The others collect pine boughs and ignite them with smouldering embers, which have been brought along expressly for this purpose in a cup-shaped blob of soft clay.

At last the moment comes. The hunters heave the flaming branches into the cave one by one. An ominous rumble emanates from the darkness, followed by a series of snorts. Stones clatter within as the bear stirs into action. On either side of the cave mouth, the men hold their spears at the ready. The two hunters overhead on the ledge lift 50-pound boulders. Suddenly the animal charges out of its smoke-filled lair, snarling, its lips raised off gleaming teeth. One boulder flies past its head and bounces down the mountainside; a second one strikes the bear on its neck and knocks it off its feet. The beast is up again in an instant, but not before four sharp wooden points have been plunged into the fur and drawn out again, stained with blood. The bear rises on its hind legs, looming high over the hunters and roaring in fury. With a sweep of its broad paw, it smacks away a spear as if it were a matchstick. Lightning quick, the bear is on the weaponless hunter, catching the man's forearm in its jaws. The snapping of bones is audible above the snarls. The hunters strike frantically at the great head, lancing the eyes, ears, throat. Then one skillful thrust severs an artery, and the animal re-

Dancing around a dismembered deer placed on a ceremonial
bed of stones, Neanderthal hunters sprinkle it with red ocher,
a pigment whose color is the brown-red of blood. Fossilized
remains were uncovered with bits of ocher amidst flints
—apparently spearheads, daggers and hand axes—in a cave
near Beirut, Lebanon, leading archeologists to think that even
60,000 years ago spiritual beliefs were so advanced that
ceremonies were staged to improve the prospects for the hunt.

leases its mangling grip and slowly sags to the ground, its life draining away.

Now the men will butcher the animal and carry the meat home. Later in the year, when the hibernating animals have left their lairs, the skull will be taken to a sacred stone chest in a cave many miles away, where, according to legend, the ancestor of their people killed the first cave bear long, long ago.

The Neanderthals' stone chests of bear bones were not simply trophies, like the stuffed animal heads hanging in the dens of modern game hunters. If contemporary examples of hunting magic are any guide, the Neanderthals were up to something much more serious. Rites involving bears are still—or at least until quite recently were—performed by a number of northerly hunting peoples, stretching from Lapland across Siberia and into the arctic wilds of the New World. Certain Siberian tribes worship the bear as the mythical first man, and they make profound apologies to the animal before killing it. In other cases, the bears are considered to be intermediaries between men and the reigning spirits of the land. The Ainu hunters of northern Japan capture a cub and treat it as an honored guest through most of the year (sometimes the women even nurse the cub); then, in the winter, the bear is sacrificed at the conclusion of a long ceremony, and the Ainu men drink its blood while the presiding shaman prays to the Creator. These people believe that the spirit of the sacrificed bear will return to the forest and report the hospitality it received. Supposedly, a favorable report will persuade the forest gods to arrange for good hunting the following year.

The Neanderthals' motives for killing cave bears and preserving the skulls in stone chests can only be guessed at, but it seems likely that beliefs about the functioning of the universe were involved. Possibly these beliefs were less intricate than those of modern hunter-gatherers. And it is safe to say that the Neanderthals' hunting magic—or any of their other rites—did not spring full-blown from the brow of some primordial genius. The beliefs underlying these rites must have begun with tiny, simple-minded speculations and gradually gained momentum over a period of tens of thousands of years.

Logic suggests that art, another glorious flower of the human imagination, also started this way—and its beginnings probably occurred during Neanderthal times, for the Cro-Magnons who lived after 35,000 B.C. were already accomplished artists who created engravings, statuary and magnificent cave paintings.

The only prehistoric arts for which there can be any surviving evidence are the visual kind—painting, sculpture, engraving and so on. If music was played during Neanderthal times, it is lost forever. The Neanderthals may have been excellent singers and perhaps even imaginative dancers; dancing is an important form of expression among all hunting peoples. But what little is known about the visual art of the Neanderthals would indicate a low level of accomplishment.

By the flickering light of torches deep in a Swiss Alpine cave, Neanderthal hunters carefully position the head of a cave bear in a stone chest in which they will place six others, all facing the cave entrance. Probably the skulls were thought to possess magic power. The now extinct cave bear, a fierce creature bigger than a grizzly, was an unlikely choice for food —far easier prey was everywhere abundant—and must have been hunted predominantly for ceremonial purposes.

The Neanderthals occasionally made use of such natural pigments as red or yellow ocher and black manganese. These crop up at their sites in powder form and sometimes in pencil-shaped pieces that show signs of being rubbed on a soft surface, such as human skin or animal hides. Neanderthal men may have painted themselves before setting out on a hunt or a war mission; possibly they created visual patterns that were thought to have some supernatural power to strike fear into the enemy, bewitch animals or otherwise augment their chances of success. But no picture or pattern rendered with these pigments survives—if indeed any ever existed.

As for other possible art forms, there is no sign of a representational engraving or statue from the era of the Neanderthals. And their deposits have not yielded a single perforated tooth that might have been used in necklaces—a very common personal ornament among hunters, including the Cro-Magnons. However, there are a few tantalizing indications that the Neanderthals were beginning to sense the visual possibilities of the materials around them. A cave at Tata in Hungary has yielded a piece of ivory that had been trimmed into an oval shape, polished and then coated with ocher. At the cave of Pech de l'Azé in southern France, a Neanderthal bored a hole in an animal bone; the bone may have been an amulet of sorts. From another French cave at Arcy-sur-Cure

come a pair of oddities—two fossils of marine animals. These are very humble art objects indeed, perhaps mere curiosities, but they have no obvious utilitarian function.

Equally cryptic are the few hints of the symbolic notation that would someday blossom into writing. A few pebbles from the Neanderthal cave at Tata have grooves that may be symbolic. An ox rib from Pech de l'Azé bears a series of scratches on one side; the scratches appear in groups of two, and they do not look at all like the marks that would have been left if someone were merely cutting meat off the bone. Perhaps these scratches are doodles, lacking in meaning, but symbolic notation had to start somewhere, and it definitely existed by 30,000 years ago, when the Cro-Magnons were making crude calendars.

All of the presumptive examples of visual expression by the Neanderthals are so rudimentary and tentative as to be barely discernible, but the first step in any endeavor is the hardest. As far as is known now, the Neanderthals seem to have had no tradition in the arts or symbolism to build on and no means of sensing the magnificent future of such expression —yet they made a beginning. This beginning, like those in religion and magic, bespeaks an awakening, wondering mind. During Neanderthal times, human nature was still in the making, but its outlines were now fully visible.

Prey and Predator: An Ice-Age Bestiary

Bigger than a grizzly, the nine-foot-long cave bear was primarily an herbivore. One Austrian cave held the remains of 30,000 bears.

Neanderthal man inhabited a world dominated by large mammals—many so huge as to have made him feel pitifully small and vulnerable in their midst. For the carnivores among them he presumably was indeed toothsome prey, yet more often than not he turned the tables on the most formidable of the meat and plant eaters

alike by slaughtering them himself.

All the mammals depicted on this and the following pages lived in Europe during the ice ages, including even the giant lion (pages 116-117). The cave lion and the cave bear favored the same kind of rock shelters that Neanderthal man might want for his own home. But there is very little

evidence that in either the competition for living space or the vital struggle for food Neanderthals contributed to the extinction of any of these huge species. Rather, the change in climate and habitats that came about with the waning of the glaciers seems to have caused most of the ice-age giants to disappear from Europe.

The scruffy cave hyena evolved in tropical India about a million years ago and spread to Europe where, judging by the profusion of its fossilized bones, it seems to have been one of the most numerous mammals of the ice age. Although the cave hyena died out in Europe, a smaller descendant, the spotted hyena, still scavenges on the savannas of Africa.

Probably the biggest cat that ever lived—at least 25 per cent larger than today's African lion—the cave lion often hunted its prey in prides as modern lions do. It was common in Europe during Neanderthal times, and a close relative survived until 5,000 to 6,000 years ago in Asia Minor.

With a thick coat and low-slung head, the woolly rhinoceros was perfectly built for a life spent grazing the stubby vegetation of the tundra near the edge of the glaciers. Its front horn, about three feet long, served as a weapon and a snow shovel for winter foraging.

The hefty, 12-foot-long aurochs was the ancestor of all domestic cattle but, unlike its mild-mannered descendants, was a formidable creature. Intensively hunted by men of ancient and modern times, the aurochs survived in central Europe until the early 17th Century.

Sporting horns up to four feet wide, this bison grazed the grasslands of Europe in enormous herds during the ice age. Its numbers seem to have declined when its habitat changed into woodlands after the climate warmed, and the species finally disappeared from Europe 10,000 years ago.

The eight-ton, 12-foot-tall woolly mammoth was ideally suited to the rigors of ice-age Europe. Shaggy hair and a layer of fat insulated it from the cold, and its ears were small to reduce heat loss. But such specializations probably proved to be its undoing: like the woolly rhinoceros, the woolly mammoth disappeared about 10,000 years ago, presumably unable to adapt to the increasingly temperate climate of its last home, the grazing grounds in Siberia and North America.

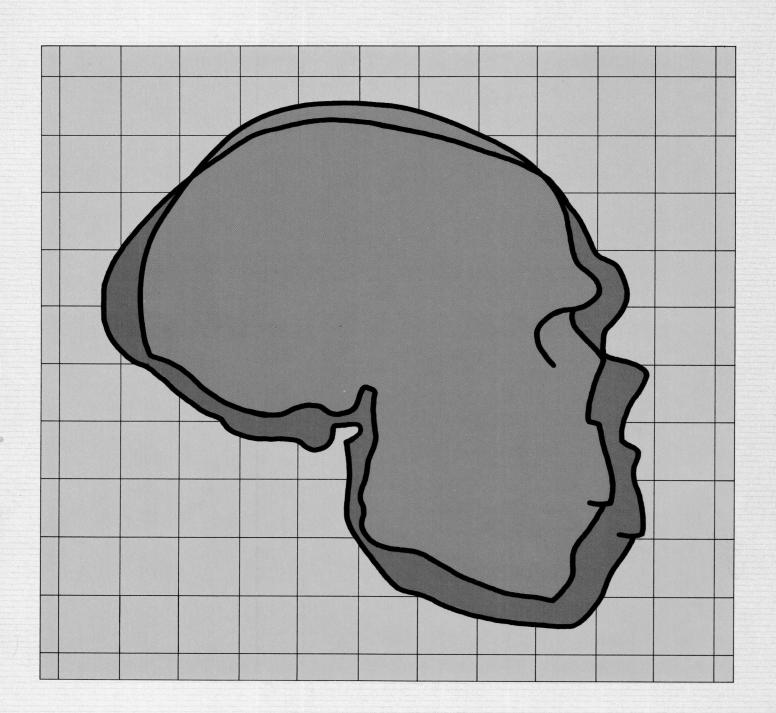

Has anybody ever seen a living Neanderthal?

Consider the following episode. One April evening in 1907, a caravan led by a Russian explorer named Porshnyev Baradiin was preparing to make camp in a central Asian desert. All day the travelers had been crossing a bleak land of rock and sand, as silent and empty as any place on earth. Now the siege of solitude was deepening, for the sun hung at the horizon, and a hint of the nighttime chill of the desert had already crept into the air. Suddenly a member of the group uttered a startled cry. He pointed to the crest of the ridge just ahead. There, silhouetted against the setting sun, stood a huge slouching figure resembling a cross between a man and an ape. For a long moment, the shaggy brute stared back. Then it turned and lumbered off in the opposite direction. The travelers gave chase but were soon outdistanced. They drifted back to the camp in a disturbed mood, comforted only by the thought that the creature's fright seemed greater than their own.

This encounter was the first recorded meeting between Westerners and one of the strange Asian beastmen known as Yetis or Abominable Snowmen. In 1921, a near-miss was reported by an English mountain climber, Colonel Howard Bury, who spotted some enormous footprints in the snow during a reconnaissance of Mount Everest. The colonel's story received far more publicity than Baradiin's did, and

The Neanderthals' anatomical diversity, which suggests they could have evolved into modern types, is seen in these two superimposed skulls. The older skull (red), from La Chapelle, France, is heavy-boned, with a sloping brow, a receding chin and a protruding "bun" at the back. By contrast, "Skhul V" (orange), from Mount Carmel in Israel, is nearly modern; smaller, with a definite chin and a high forehead, it resembles the skulls of Neanderthals' successors, the Cro-Magnons.

it seems to have started something of a fad, for dozens of similar reports have cropped up since then.

Outside of Russia, most scientists have been cool toward the Abominable Snowmen. Some Soviet scientists, however, take the reports quite seriously, and they have compiled a thick dossier on the subject, relying mainly on descriptions by Mongol caravan drivers and wandering Tibetan monks, who supposedly have had considerable contact with the creatures. The basic "facts" are these: the Abominable Snowmen walk with bent knees; they have large jaws and sloping foreheads; their naked, stooped bodies are sparsely covered by coarse reddish hair; they cannot speak, uttering only animal cries; and they subsist on a diet of small game and roots.

A few Soviet anthropologists feel that enough is known about the Abominable Snowmen to indicate their real identity: they are the last surviving Neanderthals. Presumably these half-human relics of the ice age have managed to hang on in the Asian heartland because the harsh climate suits their tastes and, more important, because ordinary mortals do not covet the region enough to kill them off.

Despite the high entertainment-quotient of this theory, its merits are slim. Hearsay about outsized footprints in the snow or giant figures disappearing behind crags is suspect. And no trustworthy photograph has ever been produced for scientific scrutiny, much less an Abominable Snowman in the flesh. Hence the creature must be accorded the doubtful status of the Loch Ness monster.

In any case, it makes little sense to link such a cringing, shuffling chimera with the Neanderthals, who stood fully upright, wore clothes and were very capable hunters. The Neanderthals are, in fact, long gone. They vanished from the face of the earth sometime around 40,000 years ago and were replaced by a new sort of human, known as Cro-Magnon man. Fully modern in physique, he rates our own taxonomic title, *Homo sapiens sapiens*. His takeover of the world was total, for none but Homo sapiens sapiens fossils have ever been found in geological deposits more recent than 40,000 B.C.

The disappearance of the Neanderthals seems to have the makings of a soul-stirring play, with the world as a stage, and the happiest ending imaginable —the ascendancy of ourselves. The only trouble is that no one really knows what happened. The actors performed behind a lowered curtain, and all anyone has been allowed to see is the beginning and end. The twists and turns of the drama that brought about the replacement of the Neanderthals constitute the greatest of all prehistoric mysteries.

A number of possible plot lines have been proposed for the middle acts. Some anthropologists believe that many—but not by any means all—Neanderthals evolved into modern men. Others make no exceptions and feel that all Neanderthals evolved into modern men. And still others—a minority nowadays—insist that all Neanderthals became extinct and were replaced by modern men who had evolved from an unknown genetic stock in an unlocated Eden. One scientist likens the problem of trying to determine the genetic connection between Neanderthals and Cro-Magnons to tracing the connection between buggies and automobiles on the basis of hubcaps and broken wheels. Actually, the most abundant evidence —stone tools—is even less direct than that, although it is highly suggestive.

Only a few years ago, textbooks used to cite the sequence of tool-bearing layers in caves and rock shelters as absolute proof that all Neanderthals became extinct. It was thought that the tools made by Neanderthals declined in number and quality as the end of their period neared; then no tools were made at all, resulting in "sterile" layers, with no sign of human habitation; then brand-new styles of tools abruptly began. What could such a sequence mean? Using the earlier analogy of stone tools as a radio broadcast across the years, imagine the following chain of events: the one station the receiver picks up has an announcer chatting away about normal topics in his normal tone of voice; suddenly he begins to sputter and yell; then he goes off the air altogether, and the radio is ominously silent for a moment; then a new voice comes on the air, talking rapidly in a totally different language. It would be only natural to assume that the radio station had been attacked and taken over by invaders.

Although an off-and-on sequence of tool-bearing strata—Neanderthal layers fading to sterile layers that are followed by Cro-Magnon layers—is indeed found at some Neanderthal sites, archeologists have begun to discover many exceptions to the old rule. At some sites, successively later layers show that toolmaking proficiency rose, rather than declined. Also, sterile layers do not always appear between Neanderthal and Cro-Magnon tools; more often, there is no break, indicating that occupation of the site was virtually continuous. And, finally, the difference between Neanderthal and Cro-Magnon tools does not necessarily indicate that one culture disappeared to be replaced by an unrelated one. This last fact may hold the key to the Neanderthal mystery, for closer study of the differences between tools could show

Making the Most of Stone

How successive improvements in toolmaking methods increased the efficiency of prehistoric craftsmen—and freed men of dependence on nearby stone supplies for tools—is shown in this chart. Each part of the spiral stands for inches of cutting edge produced from a pound of flint. The two earliest techniques, Abbevillian (*blue*) and Acheulean (*green*), gave Homo erectus only two to eight inches of cutting edge out of a pound. But with the Mousterian flake-trimming technique (*brown*), Neanderthals could obtain at least five times as much working edge per pound—40 inches in all. And their Cro-Magnon successors, employing the intricate Magdalenian method of making long thin blades, converted a pound of flint into 40 feet of cutting edge.

how Neanderthals, far from being replaced by Cro-Magnons, actually evolved into them.

The tools associated with Neanderthal peoples all over the world are called Middle Paleolithic, a word derived from the Greek *paleo* (old) and *lith* (stone); the term is a broad one that covers Mousterian tools as well as other types in eastern Asia, Africa and elsewhere. The comparable broad-gauge term for tools associated with the Cro-Magnon phase of human evolution is Upper Paleolithic ("upper" because these tools appear in layers lying on top of the earlier tools). Most Middle Paleolithic tools consist of flat flakes of stone that were knocked off a specially prepared core of flint, quartzite, chert or some other fine-grained rock and then further shaped and retouched to provide the desired working edge. Upper Paleolithic toolmakers produced flakes too—but a special kind known as blades, defined as flakes that are at least two times as long as they are wide. This shift in the fundamental unit of the tool kit is marked enough so that many collections of Middle and Upper Paleolithic tools can be distinguished at a glance.

Blades are more economical to make than flakes because they yield more than five times as much cutting edge per pound of stone. Progress is also apparent in craftsmanship. The Upper Paleolithic tools are more finely made, requiring extremely precise chipping to produce the desired point, notch or cutting edge. And there are many more kinds of special-purpose tools. Upper Paleolithic kits often include a high percentage of burins—chisellike tools useful for cutting bone, antler and ivory. Neanderthals made fewer burins and presumably were not as well equipped to exploit such materials.

Without a doubt, Upper Paleolithic tools are su-perior to those made by the Neanderthals. It seems equally clear that the changeover occurred very quickly. Earlier generations of anthropologists, work-ing under the assumption that the Neanderthals belonged to a separate species of mankind almost un-related to Cro-Magnon, naturally saw the changes in stone tools as proof that the Cro-Magnons moved in and took over. But now that the Neanderthals seem genetically closer to the Cro-Magnons, scientists are beginning to wonder if the shift can be explained by a rapid evolution of tools rather than the arrival of a new culture. If Upper Paleolithic implements devel-oped out of Middle Paleolithic styles of stonework-ing, the transition would presumably be indicated by some tools that display characteristics of both types. Now, after years of speculation, such telltale evidence of a transition has indeed appeared.

In southwest France, the two earliest Upper Paleolithic tool types are called Perigordian and Aurignacian. The Aurignacian is so utterly unlike any indigenous Middle Paleolithic style that it almost certainly was imported to western Europe by the Cro-Magnons. Tools resembling the Aurignacian have been unearthed in eastern Europe, suggesting that the immigrants came from there.

The Perigordian style of Upper Paleolithic tools is another story. Despite some claims that it is an import from the east, more and more evidence supports a local origin. It seems to have grown directly out of the Mousterian of Acheulean tradition of toolmaking —the most complex and ingenious of all Middle Paleolithic Mousterian types. At a number of sites in Europe, successive Mousterian layers dated near the end of the Neanderthals' time show a steady increase in the ratio of blades to flakes. The frequency of certain favorite Upper Paleolithic tools, such as burins, also rises. The shift is gradual, and there is no discontinuity that indicates one culture or people came to an end and were abruptly replaced.

Evidence for indigenous evolution of the Upper Paleolithic out of the Middle Paleolithic has also been found at some sites in eastern Europe, Asia and Africa, but most archeologists are steering clear of generalizations until the evidence has been more thoroughly analyzed. The truth is that no one really knows how toolmaking traditions change. Are innovations spread by migrations, barter, conquests, word of mouth, or by intermarriage between neighboring bands? Are changes spurred by rising intelligence, increasing linguistic capability or some other factor not even guessed at?

Fossils might provide a more direct line of inquiry than tools into the fate of the Neanderthals—provided enough could be found. If there were a complete series of fossils from all over the world dated from about 30,000 to 50,000 years ago, any amateur could study the remains and tell what happened to the Neanderthals. Regrettably, the trail of humanity through this period is not at all well-marked by bones. No Neanderthal fossil has been given a reliable date more recent than 40,000 years ago. The oldest securely dated modern men come from Czechoslovakia; they lived about 26,000 years ago. A few other fossils may belong in the intervening millennia, but their dates have not yet been fixed. There is a fossil gap, and it holds secure the Neanderthal mystery.

The unaccounted-for time period poses no real mystery by itself, for the world was certainly fully populated throughout the period. But populated by whom? On one side were the Neanderthals, modern in body but still rather apish above the neck, relatively clumsy in technological skills. On the other side of the gap are the Cro-Magnons, modern from head to toe, talented as artists and initiators of the idea of writing. Are these striking differences between Neanderthals and Cro-Magnons simply a result of their separation in time? And if so, how did human evolution cross the gap so fast, and where, and when, and why?

The first step in attempting to trace human evolution through this fascinating 15,000-year period is to measure the physical difference between Neanderthals and Cro-Magnons—a procedure that is not as easy as it sounds. When two extreme fossil examples are viewed side by side—for example, the man from La Chapelle-aux-Saints and the original Cro-Magnon man—the difference seems tremendous. The Neanderthal has a very long, low cranium, bulging at the sides, with a protruding "bun" at the rear of the skull, a slanting forehead and a heavy brow ridge. The Cro-Magnon has a high cranium, rounded at the rear, vertical at the sides, with a vertical forehead and no brow ridge to speak of. The faces are quite dissimilar, too. The Neanderthal has an outthrust face, a broader nose and a large, chinless jaw. By contrast, the face of the Cro-Magnon, with its regular features, could almost belong to a Hollywood leading man.

But these are the extremes. Some other Neanderthals have definite chins, rather high-vaulted craniums, little sign of a bun at the back of the skull, fairly steep foreheads and only a moderate brow ridge. And some Cro-Magnons have a rather pronounced brow ridge, sloping foreheads and large jaws.

Visual comparison of fossils is such a fallible ap-

More Work for Better Tools

Early man's steady progress in the manufacture of flint tools is traced in this diagram, which shows how increasing numbers of blows *(dots)* and different steps *(clusters of dots)* in toolmaking led to finer tools and more efficient utilization of the raw material. The most primitive tool required 25 blows and one step, while the latest and most sophisticated took 251 blows and nine complex steps, involving the hand, brain and eye of a master stone artisan.

The first and second tools below, representing the Abbevillian and Acheulean toolmaking techniques of Homo erectus, were rough-hewn from single pieces of flint. The third was made in Neanderthal times by the Mousterian technique, which involved chipping a flake from a core and then modifying the flake. And the bottom tool—a knife so sharp one edge had to be dulled to permit grasping—was shaped by the more intricate Aurignacian technique of Cro-Magnon man.

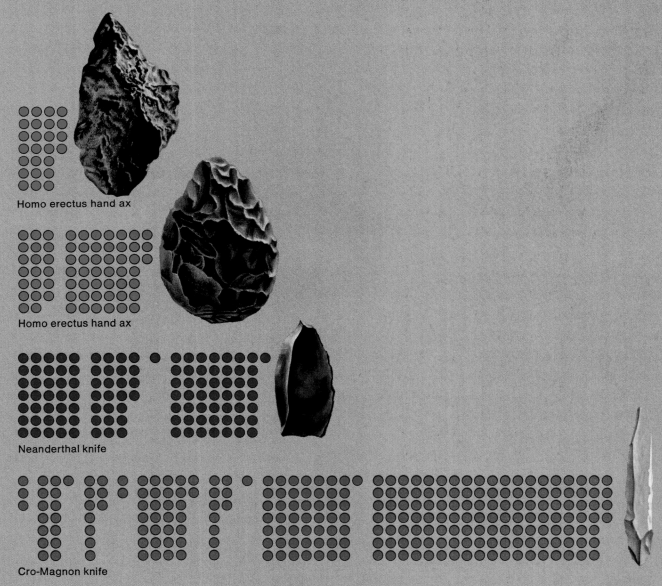

Homo erectus hand ax

Homo erectus hand ax

Neanderthal knife

Cro-Magnon knife

proach that anthropologists have been resorting more and more to statistical comparisons of tooth size, cranial height, brow formation and so on. These efforts have gone a long way toward dispelling the old impression that Neanderthals had strayed far from the mainstream of human evolution. The range of variability of Neanderthal features has been shown to overlap with the modern range of variability more so than once was thought. This means that Neanderthal features may occasionally be seen just by strolling through the nearest crowd, although no individual will have a complete array of Neanderthal characteristics. Statistical analyses have also indicated that the range of variability within Neanderthal populations was as great as among Homo sapiens sapiens. In the past, most authorities believed that the Neanderthals—especially those of western Europe —were remarkably homogeneous. Their alleged lack of variety was interpreted to mean that they had somehow lost evolutionary flexibility and had become specialized—hence, a dead end.

It helps to know that Neanderthals came in many shapes and sizes, and that these are sometimes matched by modern men. Statistics have not yet given a clear-cut answer on the key question of whether or not the evolutionary gap was crossed by a steady progression of changes, each so small as to be imperceptible yet adding up to the differences between Neanderthals and Cro-Magnons. But the current feeling among anthropologists is that this is indeed what happened: most Neanderthal populations in the world were ancestors of Homo sapiens sapiens peoples. Here is a brief, region-by-region summary of the skeletal material supporting this belief:

• In the Middle East, an ancestral relationship between the local Neanderthals and the local Cro-Magnons seems probable. This is the only locality where excellent candidates for an intermediate type of man have appeared. Some fossils from Skhul and Qafzeh in Israel seem to have a foot—or rather a skull —in both the Neanderthal and Cro-Magnon camps. The skulls display a fairly even blend of archaic and modern traits. A few experts continue to reject the idea that these Middle Eastern specimens fit on a direct line between the Neanderthals and Cro-Magnons. William Howells of Harvard, for one, classes the Skhul fossils as early Homo sapiens sapiens —Cro-Magnon types—but he considers them to be so distinct from Neanderthals as to rule out any direct relationship. His is a minority opinion, however.

• In eastern Europe, an ancestral relationship seems entirely possible, since the most recent Neanderthals appear to have been rather advanced. In addition, an intermediate-looking upper jaw has been found.

• In Southeast Asia, an ancestral relationship also seems possible, because new fossils turning up in Australia hint at an evolutionary link between Solo man, an early Neanderthal from Java, and the most ancient fossils of Australian aborigines, who were full-fledged Homo sapiens sapiens.

• In Africa, transitional specimens are lacking. However, a number of rugged-looking Homo sapiens sapiens have turned up in eastern and southern Africa. These modern men may be more than 40,000 years old, although their dates—and those for the local Neanderthals known as Rhodesian man—are still imprecise. An ancestral relationship between the two types is considered possible, and some anthropologists even feel that African Neanderthals were the first to cross the threshold to modernity.

One area—western Europe—has been left off this list of places where the evolution of Neanderthals into modern men is generally regarded as possible or probable. Western Europe is known as one of the richest fossil fields in all the world, and it has been scoured assiduously for more than a century. Yet no fossil intermediate between the local Neanderthals and Cro-Magnons has ever been found there. Since no fossil comes even close to fitting into the middle ground, most scientists are inclined to shut the western European Neanderthals out of the direct line leading to modern man. Agreement on this is far from universal, however.

C. Loring Brace of the University of Michigan, among others, believes there is no justification for treating western European Neanderthals differently. Brace feels they showed definite signs of evolving in a Cro-Magnon direction. In his opinion, the fact that their progressive tendencies look muted could be due to their antiquity. Brace suggests they may be older than is believed. No well-preserved fossil from the region can be reliably dated, since most were dug up earlier in this century, when excavation and dating techniques were crude. Some recent studies suggest that the fossils from La Ferrassie, La Chapelle-aux-Saints, Monte Circeo and elsewhere are at least 60,000 years old—an age that would lend credence to Brace's point that the local Neanderthals had plenty of time in which to evolve a modern appearance.

However, a good case can be made for the opposition viewpoint that western European Neanderthals missed the turn toward modernity and later died out. Geological factors may have influenced their fate. During certain severe cold phases of the Würm glaciation, the Scandinavian and Alpine ice sheets pushed toward each other and came within 300 miles of meeting in Germany. Neanderthals trapped behind the glaciers might have been more or less isolated from the evolutionary advances occurring elsewhere in the world. Although the isolation would have been neither total nor permanent, such geographic features could have operated as a fine-mesh genetic screen, keeping east-west contacts few. The people of western Europe might have periodically pursued an independent evolutionary course.

If these people were indeed an evolutionary dead end, what accounts for their demise? The usual answer is that invading Cro-Magnons from the east exterminated the western Neanderthals. Some anthropologists speculate that the Neanderthals were in no condition to resist when—and if—the invaders arrived. Fossil evidence indicates that many western European Neanderthals suffered from rickets, caused by a lack of vitamin D. The necessity of wearing clothes in the cold climate would have prevented natural production of this "sunshine vitamin," and the Neanderthals may not have eaten enough of the shellfish or other foods that would have made up the vitamin deficiency. But rickets could not account for the death of hundreds of thousands of people, many of whom lived in fairly mild climates. Since disease is not an adequate explanation for their disappearance, certain experts have conjured up the specter of ecological catastrophe, proposing that the local Neanderthals were so inflexibly adapted to cold that they could not handle the long warm spell that began around 38,000 years ago and lasted for 10,000 years. This notion makes little sense, however, because the Neanderthals were living in warm areas elsewhere and had thrived during earlier warm spells.

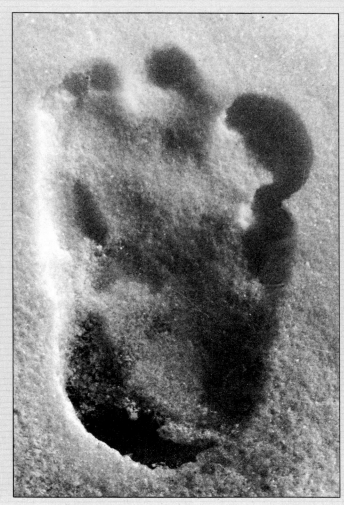

The human characteristics of a
Neanderthal footprint (above) from
a cave in Italy suggest Neanderthal was
evolving into modern man—and
was not, as some people thought, an
offshoot that lingered on as the
Abominable Snowman, or Yeti,
reported from the Himalayas. The
purported track of a Snowman, at right,
is quite unlike the Neanderthal's.

A more persuasive explanation for the death of the western European Neanderthals at the hands of invading Cro-Magnons involves linguistic ability. If the local Neanderthals could not communicate as well as an invading people, they would have been at a tremendous competitive disadvantage—one that would drastically reduce their chances of survival. The analysis of the reconstructed vocal tract of the fossil from La Chapelle-aux-Saints by Philip Lieberman and Edmund Crelin provides experimental support for this idea (Chapter Three). They estimate that, owing to the lack of a well-developed pharynx, the sound-resonating chamber at the top of the throat, the Neanderthals of western Europe may have had only 10 per cent of the speaking ability of modern man. Studies of the speaking abilities of other groups suggest that the African Neanderthals had a somewhat more highly evolved pharynx and that the advanced-looking Neanderthals of the Middle East had an almost completely modern vocal tract.

The Lieberman-Crelin hypothesis of linguistic deficiency, though widely challenged, seems the most credible doomsday factor for the western European Neanderthals. The debate is bound to continue for years, since the evidence of stone tools strongly suggests an indigenous cultural linkage between Neanderthals and Cro-Magnons. And in any case, even if the local people were overwhelmed by invaders, some intermarriage must have taken place. It is not likely that the genes of the western European Neanderthals disappeared entirely from humankind.

A fundamental question remains. If most of the Neanderthals evolved into the Cro-Magnons, why did such a change take place? What evolutionary forces could possibly explain the swift remodeling of the human skull from the form that had characterized men since Homo erectus times, a quarter of a million years or so before? Until that question is firmly answered, the transformation of the Neanderthals into modern men will be a plot without a motive.

One hypothesis directed to this problem focuses on the Neanderthal face. Anyone seeing a Neanderthal skull for the first time would be struck by the appearance of the face. It is long and decidedly outthrust. What conceivable purpose could such a facial structure serve? Dr. Brace feels that the Neanderthal teeth hold the key. He views the large, prognathous face as a supporting structure for the front teeth, which were very large. According to Brace, the size of the front teeth was a kind of technological adaptation. He thinks that Neanderthals regularly used their front teeth as a built-in tool, serving as pliers to hold one end of some material such as wood or hide so that one hand would be free to cut, scrape or pierce the material with a stone implement. Wear patterns on the incisors of some fossils suggest that the Neanderthals softened animal hides by chewing them; workers may also have twisted plant fibers or straightened wooden shafts with the aid of their teeth. All such work would favor big, strong front teeth.

To provide room for these, the face had to extend well out. Furthermore, the jaw had to be large and thick in order to withstand the stresses generated when the teeth were used as gripping, tearing or hide-softening tools. Other skull features may have been affected, too. Possibly the heavy brow ridge of the Neanderthals functioned as a sort of architectural truss to take up chewing stresses. Perhaps even the shape of the back of the skull was dictated by the massive tooth-bearing structures up front. The bun-like extension of the rear of many Neanderthal skulls may have acted to balance the outthrust face, distributing the weight of the head evenly on its supporting point at the top of the spine. Another conceivable reason for the elongated skull concerns rotary motion. The head is swiveled from side to side by means of muscles attached to the back of the head. Extension of this area, in effect, gives the muscles a longer lever arm to work with, lightening the task of moving the heavy, forward-jutting face. In other words, the bun allowed the big-faced Neanderthal to turn his head quickly.

Why would the skull evolve into its modern form? Brace feels that improvements in stone implements caused the Neanderthals to rely less and less on their front teeth as a built-in tool, leading to a gradual reduction in tooth size. This reduction, in turn, would lead to a reduction in the jaw, face and other features, giving rise to men with heads like ours.

Many scientists feel that Brace's hypothesis cannot adequately account for the transformation of the Neanderthals into men of modern appearance, and they offer alternatives. David Pilbeam, a physical anthropologist at Yale, proposed another sort of evolutionary mechanism that might have brought about the changes in the human skull. Expanding on the Lieberman-Crelin hypothesis, Pilbeam suggests that—with the possible exception of western European Neanderthals—the Neanderthal head gradually became more modern in form because of the evolution of the upper part of the throat into a pharynx capable of producing the full range of modern vocalizations. As Crelin and Lieberman pointed out, the

development of a pharynx in man can be traced by studying newborn infants—who lack complete pharynges. When this essential part of the vocal tract starts to take on its final shape at the age of three months, the larynx (or voice box) drops down in the throat, and the base of the skull, which is rather flat at birth, becomes arched. The pharyngeal space is thus formed in front of the topmost vertebrae, and the arch in the base of the skull serves as a roof.

Pilbeam believes that the evolution of the pharynx's arched roof may have affected the overall structure of the human skull. As the arch formed, the base of the skull increasingly shortened. (Imagine picking up a piece of cloth in the middle: it becomes shorter.) If the starting point for this process were a long, low Neanderthal skull, the shortening of the skull base might have caused the facial region to pull inward from its formerly outthrust position. With the face thus pulled in, the whole brain case would have had to become higher in order to pack in the same amount of brain tissue. And as this happened, the brow and the sides of the skull would have become more vertical. Thus, the Neanderthal skull was transformed into a Homo sapiens sapiens skull. Neanderthal and modern-type skulls are, in effect, just different ways of packing the same quantity of brain tissue. The overall shape of the package is dictated by only one of its dimensions—the length of the base of the skull—which is in turn dictated by the presence of a modern pharynx.

Pilbeam's logical chain of events has the great virtue of accounting for the sheer velocity of the evolutionary changes that turned Neanderthals into Cro-Magnons. The development of a pharynx could have occurred very rapidly, since speech is an incalculably valuable asset. Natural selection would have worked at maximum efficiency to weed out the slow talkers and foster better speaking ability —whereas changes in teeth or noses probably would not have gone forward at the same rapid pace. It is almost possible today, tens of thousands of years later, to sense the powerful and urgent evolutionary pressures that would have been launched when this new element was introduced into the vocal tract. The development of a modern pharynx, with its huge potential for communication, could very well explain a quantum leap in physical and cultural evolution.

Much has been learned of the pivotal period between Neanderthal and Cro-Magnon times, and much remains to be learned. Hardly any relevant fossil evidence is available from some crucial areas of the world—Arabia, located at the crossroads of two continents; the endless reaches of central Asia; and the subcontinent of India, bursting with game and blessed with the sort of warm climate that early man favored for millions of years. Nor can anthropologists say when the transformation of the Neanderthals started. Perhaps some modern-looking individuals began to appear in Neanderthal populations 50,000 or even 60,000 years ago.

Whenever and wherever it began, the evolutionary transition probably affected almost all of humankind. From the savannas of Africa to the hills of Czechoslovakia and eastward to China, men were joined in a single enormous gene pool—a great mixing vat in which traits of appearance or behavior could be exchanged by intermarriage among neighboring bands of hunter-gatherers. Because the tradition of intermarriage was apparently long established by this time, an evolutionary surge in one place eventually made itself felt everywhere else in the common gene pool, and the vast atomized horde of humankind climbed toward modernity as a single unit. By 30,000 years ago the changes were largely complete, and the world was populated with men that looked like ourselves. People were living in larger bands than they ever had before. Cultures were branching and rebranching along countless idiosyncratic paths, like a plant long in the shade suddenly offered the full strength of the sun. Successful initiatives in technology or art or symbolmaking begat more initiatives, and cultural change steadily accelerated.

The story of the Neanderthals should rightly end in the transitional period—about 35,000 or 40,000 years ago. Imagine a typical man of the time (if such a thing as a typical man can ever be said to exist). Give him an intermediate head, with a fairly high cranium, a jaw that would look only mildly outsized on a man of today, and a bit of brow ridge. Endow him with an intelligence just about equivalent to the modern level, even though his verbal communication may be less efficient than that of modern man. Place him in a landscape of tall, waving grass, with the sun shining down and the bubbling music of summer in the air. Who is this man? He is an evolutionary bridge, just shy of fully modern status. His technology marks the end of a very ancient tradition of flake tools, and his hunting-gathering way of life is not much different from that of men who lived hundreds of thousands of years earlier. But he is no shambling ape-man, as nearly everyone thought until fairly recently. He is a true human—our ancestor. We should regard him with honor, because almost everything that we are springs directly from him.

Tracking Down
the Flower People

The heavy-browed, 45,000-year-old skull of a Neanderthal man glowers from the earth in which it was found in a cave in Iraq.

Sometimes an archeological dig is like a detective story in which a sleuth starts looking for a pickpocket and ends up catching a bank robber. So it happened when Ralph Solecki organized an excavation of Shanidar Cave in northern Iraq in 1951.

Solecki, then a 34-year-old archeologist at the Smithsonian Institution,

set out to look for ancient stone tools. But by the time he was through with his work, nine years later, he had unearthed one of the largest collections of Neanderthal skeletons ever found in one place. Eight years afterward, a new analysis of his finds, carried out thousands of miles from Shanidar Cave, would reveal the Neanderthals'

symbolic use of flowers to mourn the death of one of their own—and would help change the world's view of these archaic people.

The story of this adventure, set in an exotic land and peopled by a romantic cast, is told on the following pages in pictures from Solecki's personal photo album.

Ralph Solecki and an Iraqi official began their fruitful project in May 1951, with a month-long exploration of the rugged Zagros Mountains of northern Iraq. Searching for a site that might conceal evidence of prehistoric man, Solecki and his companion prowled and poked in one cave after another —some 40 in all—finding them all either so small, so dank or so rocky that they seemed unlikely dwelling places for men in any age.

Solecki then turned to the mountain people for clues to a promising site. The local inhabitants were Kurds, native to a large area near the junction of Iraq, Iran and Turkey. Some are settled in villages, some are seminomadic, migrating in spring and autumn with their sheep and goats from one grazing place to another; they know the geography of Kurdistan as no foreigner can. Several of these shepherds guided Solecki to "Shkaft Mazin Shanidar," the Kurdish phrase for the Big Cave of Shanidar.

Solecki found the cave on Baradost Mountain above the Greater Zab River. It met all the archeologist's specifications. Huge and airy—its mouth gaped 26 feet high and 82 feet wide —it faced south and was lighted and warmed by the sun. Its floor was of earth, not stone, suggesting that prehistoric treasure could well be buried there. All in all, it was, in Solecki's words, "the most magnificent cave we had seen in our entire survey."

A nomadic Kurdish family, encountered by Solecki in his search, reposes under its goat-hair tent.

Used by migrant Kurds, a makeshift bridge spans the Greater Zab River a half mile from Shanidar.

Dotted with scrub oaks, Baradost Mountain is pierced by caves, the largest of which is Shanidar Cave, where Solecki decided to start his dig.

Solecki's conclusion that Shanidar Cave was a likely place for human habitation was proved when he took a good look inside. People were still living in the cave. Against the side walls were several lean-to huts whose Shirwani Kurdish owners had left for the summer months to graze their flocks elsewhere.

Solecki, encouraged by this evidence, recruited four men from Shanidar village and started digging in October 1951. The workers spoke no English, and Solecki's Kurdish consisted only of such essentials as the words for "flint," "bone," "money" and "payroll." Still the group worked harmoniously together, and within a few weeks had dug a test trench 43 feet long. At a depth of five feet, they turned up their first signs of prehistoric occupation: flints and flecks of charcoal from ancient hearths. While these had been left by modern men, who had occupied the cave 10,000 years ago, they were a tantalizing preview of the finds that might be revealed by additional digging.

A rude shelter stands at the rear of Shanidar—home of a migratory family that still winters there.

The Kurdish village where Solecki enlisted his workmen is a jumble of mud and stone houses.

Solecki lines up with turbaned diggers for a picture.

Workers "sign" on the payroll with their fingerprints.

Digging a test trench, workmen are careful not to disturb a Shirwani hut at the rear.

The huge excavation Solecki planned got underway in 1953. It called for quantities of equipment, and getting this material to the cave was a major problem. No regular road came near the cave, so Solecki converted the local police station located at the foot of the mountain into a temporary headquarters, home and supply depot. From here all the necessary equipment for the excavation—ropes, extension ladders and earth-screening sieves, as well as hammers, crowbars, picks, shovels, trowels, buckets and a full set of surveyor's tools—had to be hand carried up a route that took a first-rate hiker one hour to climb.

By May, Solecki and his crew were ready to begin expanding and deepening the test trench. This time they set as their goal bedrock, 45 feet down. The work was backbreaking and slow, and the job seemed endless: about 1,500 tons of earth and broken stone lay between the men and rock bottom, and every ounce of it had to be meticulously combed for any evidence of man's past.

As a policeman and children watch, workers unload boxes of tools and bedding at the police post.

A work crew of equipment-burdened Kurds starts the climb to the cave along a narrow dirt path.

Trained by Solecki to glean every last flint or bone from the cave, Kurdish workmen meticulously filter the excavated soil through huge screens.

As a 30-second fuse burns, eight workmen scramble up the trench to escape a blast.

Situated near a geological fault, Shanidar has endured many earthquakes, which over the ages sent huge boulders tumbling onto the floor of the cave, there to be buried as sediment layers gradually built up. Dynamiting was the only way to extract these boulders from the trench as they were uncovered. Precautions had to be taken to make the charges small enough to fracture the rocks without damaging any surrounding buried relics —or people: routinely, Solecki and one workman remained in the pit to light the fuse and then had about 30 seconds to clamber out with help from the other workmen who had already climbed the pit's rough wall. The nimble Kurds suffered no casualties—and they even managed to lighten their dangerous work with an occasional unexpected treat *(opposite, top)*.

Bedrock was finally reached *(opposite, bottom)*, but before that goal was achieved something much more exciting happened to make all the strain and scrutiny worthwhile: on June 22, 1953, at a depth of 25 feet, a skeleton was found. First a few tiny teeth, then fragments of a little skull led Solecki to the bones of a Neanderthal infant that had been less than a year old when it died. The Shanidar baby, as it came to be called, was very small and its tiny bones were mostly rotted, but the skeleton offered tangible evidence that Shanidar Cave had indeed been a home to men for at least 60,000 years.

A porcupine that fell into the pit will become kabob.

A worker at bottom takes the trench's depth: 45 feet.

A surveyor's marking pin measures the 15-inch Shanidar baby still embedded in soil.

Accustomed to their old bucket-brigade method of removing dirt from the dig, some workmen ignore the newly acquired automatic conveyer.

Where a Neanderthal infant lay buried, the remains of adults could not be far off. Finding them was the objective when Solecki arrived back at Shanidar in late 1956.

To help with the hunt, scientists from both Europe and America—including Solecki's archeologist wife, Rose—joined the team. The mechanics of digging and searching were modernized with new equipment that included a gasoline-powered bucket conveyer for hauling dirt and stones out of the pit. As the work proceeded on the trench, Solecki and his colleagues carefully probed at its walls with trowels and light picks.

On April 27, 1957, they found, embedded in the pit's wall at a depth of 14 feet, the skull of a man. The bones had been crushed by a heavy blow on the top of his head, probably caused by a falling boulder dislodged during a Stone Age earthquake. The skull looked, when Solecki first saw it, "like a very soiled and broken gigantic egg." Nevertheless, certain conspicuous features—the sloping forehead, heavy brow and massive jaw—caused Solecki to write in his notebook: "A Neanderthal if I ever saw one."

The unearthed skull of a man displays evidence of the heavy blow that crushed it.

A sentinel guards the Soleckis' entrance.

A guard sings to a drum accompaniment.

Life at Shanidar was not all hauling stones and brushing dirt off bones. Having become celebrities among the local Kurds, members of the Solecki team were hosted by tribal dignitaries who laid on lavish meals.

Otherwise the scientists spent their off-site time in quiet hours of work at their police-post laboratory. While Rose Solecki sorted and studied specimens that related to her own special field—archeology of a later era when agriculture was being developed—her husband and his colleagues examined the Neanderthal fossils.

Examination of the man's skull in the laboratory revealed several interesting clues about life and death in Neanderthal times. The man had died, it was clear, from a colossal whack on his head. But inspection of his skeleton showed that even when alive he had been seriously handicapped: a birth defect had denied him the use of the upper right side of his body, and he was also arthritic and blind in one eye. In short, he must have been dependent on others for food as well as protection. It was clear to Solecki that the Neanderthals had possessed the humane instinct to care for those of their fellows who could not fend for themselves.

Rose Solecki catalogues flint tools in the laboratory, a mosquito net draping the wall.

In the tent of a Kurdish chief (at left), Rose Solecki, two Iraqi officials and the headman of Shanidar village eat dinner seated on a Persian rug.

More and more skeletons were found at Shanidar, and by 1960, the last season, the total of nine Neanderthals had been unearthed. But the discovery that Solecki feels is most significant of all took place eight years later in the Paris laboratory of paleobotanist Arlette Leroi-Gourhan as she carried out a search for microscopic clues to ancient plant life in soil dug up with the fourth of the Shanidar skeletons.

When found, the skeleton did not look out of the ordinary. It was shipped off to Baghdad, mummified in cotton, papier-mâché, burlap and plaster of Paris, and crated in a coffinlike box. From Baghdad Solecki sent soil samples to Leroi-Gourhan in Paris to be examined for whatever plant-life remains they might contain.

One day in 1968 she realized that what she saw through her microscope was pollen from eight different flowers: relatives of grape hyacinth, bachelor's button, hollyhock and others. Experts agreed that the plants could not have grown in the cave or been carried there by animals. It seemed clear that the corpse had been buried with wild flowers gathered from the hillside. Here was proof that Neanderthals were loving men who confronted death with complex emotions and who mourned a loss in a ritualistic way by strewing the dead with flowers. "No longer," Solecki wrote, "can we deny the early men the full range of human feelings and emotions."

The excavation completed, an anthropologist sifts soil where a fourth skeleton was discovered.

The skeleton lies as it was, buried with wild flowers.

Solecki's colleagues cover the remains with plaster.

Straining under the weight of their load, workmen carry the remains to the laboratory.

The Emergence of Man

This chart records the progression of life on earth from its first appearance in the waters of the new-formed planet through the evolution of man; it traces his physical, social, technological and intellectual development to the Christian era. To place these advances in commonly used chronological sequences, the column

Geology	Archeology	Billions of Years Ago	
Precambrian earliest era		4.5	Creation of the Earth
		4	Formation of the primordial sea
			First life, single-celled algae and bacteria, appears in water
		3	
		2	
		1	
		Millions of Years Ago	
			First oxygen-breathing animals appear
		800	
			Primitive organisms develop interdependent specialized cells
		600	Shell-bearing multicelled invertebrate animals appear
Paleozoic ancient life			Evolution of armored fish, first animals to possess backbones
		400	Small amphibians venture onto land
			Reptiles and insects arise
			Thecodont, ancestor of dinosaurs, arises
Mesozoic middle life		200	Age of dinosaurs begins
			Birds appear
			Mammals live in shadow of dinosaurs
		100	Age of dinosaurs ends
		80	
			Prosimians, earliest primates, develop in trees
Cenozoic recent life		60	
		40	Monkeys and apes evolve
		20	
		10	Ramapithecus, oldest known primate with apparently manlike traits, evolves in India and Africa
		8	
		6	Australopithecus, closest primate ancestor to man, appears in Africa
		4	

Geology	Archeology	Millions of Years Ago	
Lower Pleistocene oldest period of most recent epoch	**Lower Paleolithic** oldest period of Old Stone Age	2	Oldest known tool fashioned by man in Africa
			First true man, Homo erectus, emerges in East Indies and Africa
		1	Homo erectus migrates throughout Old World tropics
		Thousands of Years Ago	
Middle Pleistocene middle period of most recent epoch		800	Homo erectus populates temperate zones
			Man learns to control and use fire
		600	
			Large-scale, organized elephant hunts staged in Europe
		400	Man begins to make artificial shelters from branches
		200	
Upper Pleistocene latest period of most recent epoch	**Middle Paleolithic** middle period of Old Stone Age		Neanderthal man emerges in Europe
		80	
		60	Ritual burials in Europe and Near East suggest belief in afterlife
			Woolly mammoths hunted by Neanderthals in northern Europe
		40	Cave bear becomes focus of cult in Europe
	Upper Paleolithic latest period of Old Stone Age	30	Cro-Magnon man arises in Europe
			Man reaches Australia
			Oldest known written record, a lunar calendar on bone, made in Europe
		25	Asian hunters cross Bering Strait to populate North and South America
			Figurines sculpted for nature worship
			First artists decorate walls and ceilings of caves in France and Spain
		20	Invention of needle makes sewing possible
			Bison hunting begins on Great Plains of North America
Holocene present epoch	**Mesolithic** Middle Stone Age	10	Bow and arrow invented in Europe
			Dog domesticated in North America

(Last Ice Age — vertical label spanning Upper Pleistocene through Holocene)

▼ Four billion years ago   ▼ Three billion years ago

▲ Origin of the Earth (4.5 billion)   ▲ First life (3.5 billion)

it the far left of each of the chart's four sections identifies the great geological eras into which earth history is divided, while the second column lists the archeological ages of human history. The key dates in the rise of life and of man's outstanding accomplishments appear in the third column (years and events mentioned in this volume of

The Emergence of Man appear in bold type). The chart is not to scale; the reason is made clear by the bar below, which represents in linear scale the 4.5 billion years spanned by the chart—on the scaled bar, the portion relating to the total period of known human existence (far right) is too small to be distinguished.

151

Geology	Archeology	Years B.C.	
Holocene (cont.)	Mesolithic (cont.)	9000	Jericho settled as the first town
			Sheep domesticated in Near East
	Neolithic New Stone Age		
		8000	Pottery first made in Japan
			Goat domesticated in Persia
			Man cultivates his first crops, wheat and barley, in Near East
		7000	Pattern of village life grows in Near East
			Catal Huyuk, in what is now Turkey, becomes the first trading center
			Loom invented in Near East
			Agriculture begins to replace hunting in Europe
		6000	Cattle domesticated in Near East
			Copper used in trade in Mediterranean area
	Copper Age		Corn cultivated in Mexico
		4000	Sail-propelled boats used in Egypt
			Oldest known massive stone monument built in Brittany
			First cities rise on plains of Sumer
			Cylinder seals begin to be used as marks of identification in Near East
		3500	First potatoes grown in South America
			Wheel originates in Sumer
			Egyptian merchant trading ships start to ply the Mediterranean
			First writing, pictographic, composed, Near East
		3000	Bronze first used to make tools in Near East
	Bronze Age		City life spreads to Nile Valley
			Plow is developed in Near East
			Accurate calendar based on stellar observation devised in Egypt
			Sumerians invent potter's wheel
			Silk moth domesticated in China
			Minoan navigators begin to venture into seas beyond the Mediterranean
		2600	Variety of gods and heroes glorified in *Gilgamesh* and other epics in Near East
			Pyramids built in Egypt
		2500	Cities rise in the Indus Valley

Geology	Archeology	Years B.C.	
Holocene (cont.)	Bronze Age (cont.)	2400	Stonehenge, most famous of ancient stone monuments, begun in England
			Earliest written code of laws drawn up in Sumer
		2000	Chicken and elephant domesticated in Indus Valley
			Use of bronze spreads to Europe
			Eskimo culture begins in Bering Strait area
			Man begins to cultivate rice in Far East
			Herdsmen of Central Asia learn to tame and ride horses
		1500	Invention of ocean-going outrigger canoes enables man to reach islands of South Pacific
			Oldest known paved roads built in Crete
			Ceremonial bronze sculptures created in China
			Imperial government, ruling distant provinces, established by Hittites
		1400	Iron in use in Near East
	Iron Age		First complete alphabet devised in script of the Ugarit people in Syria
			Hebrews introduce concept of monotheism
		1000	Reindeer domesticated in northern Europe
		900	Phoenicians develop modern alphabet
		800	Celtic culture begins to spread use of iron throughout Europe
			Nomads create a far-flung society based on the horse in Russian steppes
			First highway system built in Assyria
			Homer composes *Iliad* and *Odyssey*
		700	Rome founded
			Wheel barrow invented in China
		200	Epics about India's gods and heroes, the *Mahabharata* and *Ramayana*, written
			Water wheel invented in Near East
		0	Christian era begins

▼ Two billion years ago   ▼ One billion years ago

First oxygen-breathing animals (900 million) ▲   First animals to possess ▲ backbones (470 million)   First men (1.3 million) ▲

Credits

The sources for the illustrations in this book are shown below. Credits from left to right are separated by semicolons, from top to bottom by dashes.

Cover—Painting by Burt Silverman, background photograph by Ernst Haas. 8—Drawing by Hermann Schaaffhausen, Der Neanderthaler Fund, Marcus Publishers, Bonn 1888, courtesy University Library, Bonn, photographed by Edo Koenig; Reconstruction by M. Joanny-Durand under the supervision of Marcellin Boule courtesy Institut de Paléontologie Humaine, Paris, photographed by Dmitri Kessel; Reconstruction by Carleton Coon courtesy University Museum, University of Pennsylvania, photographed by Reuben Goldberg—Reconstruction by G. Wandel courtesy Dr. F. Krantz, Rheinisches Mineralien-Kontor, photographed by Edo Koenig; Reconstruction by Carleton Coon courtesy University Museum, University of Pennsylvania, photographed by Reuben Goldberg; Reconstruction by R. N. Wegner courtesy of The American Museum of Natural History—Reconstruction by M. M. Gerasimov, from the book *The Face Finder* by M. M. Gerasimov. English Translation Copyright © 1971 by Hutchinson & Co. (Publishers) Ltd. Reproduced by permission of the publishers, J. B. Lippincott Company; Reconstruction by Adolph H. Schultz courtesy the Anthropological Institute, Zurich University, photographed by Rudolf Rohr; Reconstruction by Gerhard Heberer. 12—Derek Bayes courtesy Victoria and Albert Museum, London—Culver Pictures; The Mansell Collection, London. 13—Culver Pictures; Osterreichische Nationalbibliothek—The Mansell Collection, London; Thames & Hudson *Darwin and His World*. 16—Rheinisches Landesmuseum Bonn; Staatsbibliothek Berlin; Underwood & Underwood. 17—By Permission of The Librarian, University College, Galway, Ireland; The Bettmann Archive; Roger Viollet. 21—Courtesy of Field Museum of Natural History, Chicago. 24,25—Skull courtesy University Museum, University of Pennsylvania. Sculpture by Nicholas Fasciano, photographed by Ken Kay. 29 through 37—Paintings by Herb Steinberg, background photographs are listed separately: 29,30,31—Dean Brown. 32—Bernard Wolf. 33—Dean Brown. 34,35—Bernard Wolf. 36,37—Dr. Georg Gerster from Rapho-Guillumette. 38—Map by Lowell Hess. 42,43—Lee Boltin courtesy Professor Ralph Solecki, Columbia University. 46,47—Dean Brown. 50,51—Sebastian Milito courtesy Marie-Antoinette and Henry de Lumley. 56,57—Lee Boltin courtesy Professor Ralph Solecki, Columbia University. 59,60,61—Fritz Goro courtesy Dr. Jeffrey Bada, Scripps Institution of Oceanography, University of California. 62,63—Ian Yeomans courtesy J. H. Fremlin, The University of Birmingham, Birmingham, England. 64—Erich Hartmann from Magnum courtesy Dr. T. Dale Stewart, Smithsonian Institution. 65—Brian Hesse courtesy Isabella Drew. 66—Erich Hartmann from Magnum courtesy Dr. William Farrand and Paul Goldberg, University of Michigan. 67—Paul Goldberg. 68,69—Erich Hartmann from Magnum courtesy Steve Kopper, Long Island University. 70 through 81—Drawings by Victor Lazzaro. 83—Farrell Grehan for LIFE. 84,85—Ernst Haas. 86,87—Harald Sund. 88,89—Dale Brown. 90,91—Victor Englebert from De Wys, Inc. 92,93—Harvey Lloyd from Nancy Palmer Photo Agency. 94,95—Dale A. Zimmerman and Marian Zimmerman. 96 through 113—Drawings by Herb Steinberg. 115 through 121—Paintings by Don Punchatz. 125—Drawing by George V. Kelvin. 128—Paintings by Adolph E. Brotman. 131—Courtesy Musée de l'Homme; The Mount Everest Foundation. 135 through 149—Courtesy Professor Ralph Solecki, Columbia University.

Acknowledgments

For the help given in the preparation of this book, the editors are indebted to Elaine Anderson, Assistant Curator of Paleontology, Idaho State University Museum, Pocatello; J. Lawrence Angel, Curator, Physical Anthropology, Smithsonian Institution, Washington, D.C.; Jeffrey L. Bada, Assistant Professor of Oceanography, Scripps Institution of Oceanography, University of California, La Jolla; Michael L. Bender, Professor of Oceanography, Graduate School of Oceanography, University of Rhode Island, Kingston; François Bordes, Professor of Geology, University of Bordeaux, France; C. Loring Brace, Curator of Physical Anthropology, Museum of Anthropology, University of Michigan, Ann Arbor; Ernest S. Burch Jr., Associate Professor of Anthropology, and Dr. William D. Pruitt Jr., Professor of Zoology, University of Manitoba, Winnipeg; Bernard Campbell, Professor of Anthropology, University of California, Los Angeles; J. Desmond Clark, Professor of Anthropology, University of California, Berkeley; Patricia Daly, Research Assistant, and Dexter Perkins Jr., Research Associate, Faunal Research Group, Department of Anthropology, Columbia University; Isabella M. Drew, Research Associate, Department of Anthropology, Columbia University; Rhodes W. Fairbridge, Professor of Geology, Columbia University; William R. Farrand, Associate Professor of Geology and Mineralogy, University of Michigan, Ann Arbor; J. H. Fremlin, Professor of Applied Radioactivity, Department of Physics, University of Birmingham, England; Paul Goldberg, Brooklyn, New York; Ralph L. Holloway, Associate Professor of Anthropology, Columbia University; Sidney S. Horenstein, Scientific Assistant, American Museum of Natural History, New York City; F. Clark Howell, Professor of Anthropology, University of California, Berkeley; William Howells, Professor of Anthropology, Harvard University; Arthur J. Jelinek, Professor of Anthropology, University of Arizona, Tucson; Clifford H. Jolly, Associate Professor of Anthropology, New York University; J. S. Kopper, Assistant Professor of Anthropology, Long Island University, New York; Alan Mann, Assistant Professor of Anthropology, University of Pennsylvania, Philadelphia; Professor J. R. Napier, Birbeck College, London; David R. Pilbeam, Associate Professor of Anthropology, Yale University; Keith Stammers, Department of Physics, University of Birmingham, England; T. Dale Stewart, Anthropologist Emeritus, National Museum of Natural History, Smithsonian Institution, Washington, D.C.; Richard H. Tedford, Curator of Vertebrate Paleontology, American Museum of Natural History, New York City.

Bibliography

General

Adams, Fred T., *The Way to Modern Man, An Introduction to Modern Man.* Teachers College Press, Columbia University, 1968.

Baslam, Al, *The Wonder That Was India.* Hawthorn Books, 1963.

Brace, C. Loring, *The Stages of Human Evolution.* Prentice-Hall, 1967.

Brodrick, Alan Houghton, *Man and His Ancestry.* Fawcett Publications, 1964.

Butzer, Karl W., *Environment and Archeology, An Ecological Approach to Prehistory.* Aldine-Atherton, 1971.

Coon, Carleton S.:
The Hunting Peoples. Little, Brown, 1971.
The Story of Man. Alfred A. Knopf, 1969.

Cowen, Robert C., *Frontiers of the Sea, The Story of Oceanographic Exploration.* Doubleday, 1960.

Eiseley, Loren, *Darwin's Century: Evolution and the Men Who Discovered It.* Doubleday, 1958.

Harrison, G. A., J. S. Weiner, J. M. Tanner and N. A. Barnicot, *Human Biology.* Oxford University Press, 1964.

Howell, F. Clark, *Early Man.* TIME-LIFE BOOKS, 1970.

Howells, William, *Mankind in the Making, The Story of Human Evolution.* Doubleday, 1967.

Klaatsch, Herman, M.D., *The Evolution and Progress of Mankind.* Frederick A. Stokes, 1923.

Korn, Noel, and Fred Thompson, *Human Evolution, Readings in Physical Anthropology.* Holt, Rinehart and Winston, 1967.

Kurtén, Björn, *Pleistocene Mammals of Europe.* Aldine, 1968.

Lee, Richard B., and Irven DeVore, eds., *Man the Hunter.* Aldine, 1968.

Lieberman, Philip, and Edmund S. Crelin, "On the Speech of Neanderthal Man." *Linguistic Inquiry,* Vol. II, No. 2, Spring, 1971.

Mayr, Ernst, *Populations, Species and Evolution.* The Belknap Press of Harvard University Press, 1970.

Pfeiffer, John E., *The Emergence of Man.* Harper & Row, 1969.

Sullivan, Walter, "The Life and Times of Man 200,000 Years Ago." *The New York Times,* October 17, 1971.

Tobias, Phillip V., *The Brain in Hominid Evolution.* Columbia University Press, 1971.

Wendt, Herbert, *In Search of Adam.* Collier Books, 1963.

Fossils and Tools

Bordaz, Jacques, *Tools of the Old and New Stone Age.* The Natural History Press, 1970.

Bordes, François, *The Old Stone Age.* McGraw-Hill, 1968.

Boule, Marcellin, and Henri V. Vallois, *Fossil Men.* Dryden Press, 1957.

Brace, C. Loring, Harry Nelson and Noel Korn, *Atlas of Fossil Man.* Holt, Rinehart and Winston, 1971.

Brose, David S., and Milford H. Wolpoff, "Early Upper Paleolithic Man and Late Middle Paleolithic Tools." *American Anthropologist,* Vol. 73, October, 1971.

Clark, Desmond J., *The Prehistory of Africa.* Praeger, 1970.

Flint, Richard Foster, *Glacial and Quaternary Geology.* John Wiley & Sons, 1971.

Leakey, L. S. B., and Vanne Morris Goodall, *Unveiling Man's Origins.* Schenkman, 1969.

Oakley, Kenneth, *Frameworks for Dating Fossil Man.* Aldine, 1964.

Rycraft, William Plane, *Rhodesian Man and Associated Remains.* British Museum (Natural History), 1928.

West, R. G., *Pleistocene Geology and Biology.* John Wiley & Sons, 1968.

Neanderthals

Brace, C. Loring:
"The Fate of the 'Classic' Neanderthals: A Consideration of Hominid Catastrophism." *Current Anthropology,* Vol. 5, No. 1, February, 1964.
"Ridiculed, Rejected, But Still Our Ancestor, Neanderthal." *Natural History,* May, 1968.

De Lumley, Henry, "A Paleolithic Camp at Nice." *Scientific American,* Vol. 220, No. 5, May, 1969.

Eiseley, Loren, "Neanderthal Man and the Dawn of Human Paleontology." *The Quarterly Review of Biology,* Vol. 32, No. 4, December, 1957.

Smith, G. Elliot, "Neanderthal Man Not Our Ancestor." *Scientific American,* August, 1928.

Solecki, Ralph S., *Shanidar, The First Flower People.* Alfred A. Knopf, 1971.

Weckler, J. E., "Neanderthal Man." *Scientific American,* Vol. 197, No. 6, December, 1957.

Wells, H. G., "The Grisly Folk and Their War With Men." *The Saturday Evening Post,* Vol. 193, No. 37, March 1921.

Index

Numerals in italics indicate an illustration of the subject mentioned.

Printed in U.S.A.